CAISTER
THE SEA STORY

Also by the author :-

The Beachmen

The Antiquities of King's Lynn

The Ingenious Mr Henry Bell

The Remaking of King's Lynn

The Winterton Story

CAISTER
THE SEA STORY

by

David Higgins

PHOENIX PUBLICATIONS

Published in 2010 by Phoenix Publications
18a The Howards, North Wootton,
King's Lynn, Norfolk, PE30 3RS.
Tel: 01553 679489

Origination and printing by
DSD Printers, King's Lynn, Norfolk Tel: 01553 661166.

British Library Cataloguing in Publication Data
A catalogue record for this book is available from the British Library

ISBN 978-0-9540684-4-8

Contents

Acknowledgements

I would like to express my gratitude to the following organisations and people who, in one way or another, have helped in the production of this book, including the provision of illustrations.

The Great Yarmouth Library, the Norwich Library, the Norfolk Record Office, the National Archives and the Caister Volunteer Lifeboat Service.

Peter Allard, Frank Brown, Freddy Brown, Larry Brown, Jill Carter, Jack Chase, Robert H. George, Margaret Hidden, Jim Higgins, Jack Hubbard, Charles Knights, Bob Malster, Jack Plummer, Benny Read, Billy Read, Marie Read, William Read, Colin Tooke, Parry Watson, David Woodhouse and John Skipper Woodhouse.

Jane Whiskens at D.S.D. Printers.

Special thanks are due to Derek George, who first approached me to write this book, and was very supportive thereafter and to my partner, Sheila, for encouragement, typing the manuscript and general assistance.

**This book is dedicated to all those Caister men and women
who over the years pursued a seafaring way of life.**

PREFACE

In the 1970s I became fascinated with the history of Winterton. This led me to carry out documentary research, supplemented by interviews with those in the village who still remembered 'the old days and the old ways'. During those interviews I discovered the beach companies, a term completely new to me, but when I tried to learn more about them I found that very little had been written, a situation I decided to rectify.

Shifting tack I set about researching these interesting organisations, which had existed in all the settlements between Mundesley and Aldeburgh, including Caister. There was, however, another reason why I wanted to study the village and that was that significant numbers of Winterton men had migrated there in the first half of the 19th century, all but taking over the existing seafaring work. In Caister I carried out more interviews and spent many hours, over several years, at 99 Beach Road, where Skipper Woodhouse and his brother David did all they could to further the research. The outcome was 'The Beachmen', published in 1987.

With other demands on my time I did not return to East Norfolk coastal history until 2008, when I was approached to give a talk in Winterton, in aid of the church restoration fund. Viewing this as a timely prompt I decided to use the material gathered all those years ago to produce, 'The Winterton Story'. This was launched in the village in July 2009 and has since been reprinted.

As luck would have it Derek George, the Company Secretary of the Caister Volunteer Lifeboat Service, was at the launch and afterwards asked me to consider writing a similar volume on Caister, as the two villages shared a common seafaring heritage. The idea appealed, but I was aware that, unlike Winterton, Caister already had several books written about it, including works on specific aspects, such as the lifeboats. More significantly most of the available photographs had already been published. I did feel, however, that there was one Caister tale yet to be told and that was the 'Sea Story', bringing together, in an integrated fashion, all the activities which related to the sea. The result is, 'Caister, the Sea Story'.

While this book has been written to appeal to anyone with an interest in seafaring Caister, I have tried to include, for the benefit of family historians, as many photographs as possible of named individuals and, for the boat enthusiast, a comprehensive record of Caister owned sailing boats and steam drifters. If anyone has other photographs they think might interest me I would be very pleased to hear from them.

David Higgins
April 2010

1

1. Nightwatch. Caister beachmen on the watch-house staging and stairway, 1935.

1. ORIGIN AND EARLY DAYS

Caister lies two miles north of Great Yarmouth, at the end of a straight road built as a causeway under Acts of Parliament of 1711 and 1723.[1] Its seafaring reputation is firmly rooted in the work of the beachmen who launched their yawls and lifeboats from the shore forming the eastern boundary of the parish, but this is a relatively recent orientation. For much of its early maritime history Caister had a more important southern shoreline, which greatly influenced the settlement of the area.

Caister is recorded in the early 11th century,[2] but its name points to Roman origins, with the old English *Caester* meaning a Roman camp or fort.[3] Roman material had been turning up in the parish for years, but it was Charles Green's excavations in the 1950s, that first revealed substantial structural remains, on the northern side of the Norwich Road, some 200 metres west of the parish church. Green interpreted these remains as a small port town, but subsequent excavation and reinterpretation of his work has shown that they were those of a fort with a *vicus*, or associated civilian settlement, to the west.[4]

The fort was constructed in the early 2nd century, on the south-eastern corner of an island, later to be called Flegg by the Danish settlers. In its elevated position it commanded a 'Great Estuary' to the south, the water of which flowed freely over where Yarmouth now stands. In fact open water stretched from Caister, southwards to the northern shore of Lothingland, some four miles away.

Probably called *Gariannonum* the fort was built close to a small landing place or harbour, located on a sheltered bay to the south. It is likely that naval vessels of the *Classis Britannica* operated from here, safeguarding trade routes and carrying out defensive duties. The exact purpose of the fort, at any given time, is unknown, but it later operated in conjunction with the fort, now called Burgh Castle, situated on the southern shore of the Estuary. Both were garrisoned by cavalry.

These forts were associated with a number of others located around the southern coastline of England from Brancaster, in north-west Norfolk, to Porchester, in Hampshire, all under the command of an officer called the Count of the Saxon Shore.

That the fort was on an island, with a role closely linked to the sea, makes this Roman presence the earliest phase in Caister's sea story. Perhaps Aurelius Atticianus, who fulfilled his vow to Mercury there, is the village's earliest named seafarer.[5]

The Roman Government relinquished political control over *Britannia* in the early 5th century, but by then the fort at Caister seems to have fallen into disuse. The site remained unoccupied for at least 200 years, until settled by a community of Anglo-Saxons, whose extensive cemetery was discovered by Green during his excavations, immediately south of the fort, on the opposite side of the Norwich Road.

The settlement associated with the graveyard has yet to be discovered, but it was probably within or close to the fort and the landing place. Of the 163 graves examined 12 had coffin lids made from sections of hull planking, the clench nails from which survived. In the opinion of Rainbird Clarke, 'These 'pseudo ship-burials' would appear to be a poor man's version of the pagan tradition embodied in the Sutton Hoo cenotaph and imply the derivation of the Caister community from the Ipswich region'.[6]

From the size of the cemetery and the burial density, it is estimated that there could have been anything up to 4,000 graves. The earliest burials date from the 8th century and the latest to the mid-11th century. All had a Christian orientation and it is possible that they were associated with a church, which might even have been a Minster, as the quality of the Middle-Saxon finds from

2. Robert Haylett, son of boatowner Walter Haylett, excavating the Roman fort, 1951.

3. Part of the Anglo-Saxon cemetery discovered to the south of the fort, 1954.

the fort area suggests a settlement of high status.

All this suggests that Caister is likely to have been *Cnobheresburg*, the site of Fursa's monastery, which Bede described as 'pleasantly situated near to the sea and to forests and constructed in a *castrum*'.[7]

The next wave of sea-borne settlers, the Norsemen, transformed the Flegg into a Danish Island, for of its 22 villages 13 have names ending in *by*, the old Scandinavian for village or homestead.[8] Caister retained its Anglo-Saxon name, but came under the sway of such men as Grimulf the Dane, who in 1047 left land in Caister to the Abbey of St. Benet of Holme, including a church, the earliest reference to such a building, and Thurketel Heyng who, on his death, also left land to the Abbey.[9]

In 1086, William 1, the Norman conqueror of England, ordered a survey to be taken of his kingdom and it is from the pages of this Domesday Book that the earliest insight into Caister, as a community, is to be found.[10] In all 113 men are recorded, representing the heads of households of a population of around 500 people, the largest on the Flegg.[11] These men farmed at least 720 acres with 27½ plough teams and also had access to 9½ acres of meadow. As far as livestock is concerned mention is made of 3 horses, 8 cattle, 12 pigs and 360 sheep. There was also a mill shared with the adjoining parish of Mautby, the only one mentioned for the Flegg Hundreds. It is likely that this was a watermill standing on the Pickerill Holme, the boundary between the two parishes.

The Survey also includes Yarmouth, a town of some 80 burgesses, showing that by then the Estuary was substantially blocked by the sandbank on which the town stands. That there was still a navigable northern channel to the sea is shown by the existence at Caister of a substantial salt making industry, comprising 45 salt workings, located on the parish's southern shore. Here saltwater was collected in pools and allowed to evaporate in the sun. The brine so produced was then heated in pans until all that was left was the salt. The adjoining parishes of Mautby and Runham had a significant, but lesser, number of workings, but further west they decline sharply, suggesting that suitable saltwater no longer penetrated that far inland at this time.

Leaving aside the salt industry the Domesday description of Caister is that of a simple farming community. There is no mention of fishing, but this is probably because the survey was concerned with fixed manorial economic activity, whereas fishing was more transient and open to everyone. As such it was not a direct source of manorial income, other than at Yarmouth, where 24 fishermen were recorded. It can safely be assumed that 'longshore fishing did take place at Caister at this time and had done so for centuries, as with all coastal villages.

It is difficult to say how far, if at all, 11th century Caister had moved away from the Norwich Road. The church mentioned at this time was probably on the site of the present day parish church, but this cannot be certain for the earliest known piece of church fabric, a lancet window, dates from no earlier that the 13th century. The village still retained a relationship with its southern shore, but it is possible that it had already begun to creep southwards, towards some form of crossing to and from the emerging town of Yarmouth, and eastwards towards the present day beach.

Only two manorial lords are recorded in the Domesday Survey as gaining benefit from the land and people of Caister, William I and the Abbot of St. Benet of Holme. Over the centuries these manorial holdings changed hands, were sub-let or amalgamated, passing down through such families as the de Gournays, de Castres, de Vaux, Cleres and Bardolfs until they became consolidated under the Fastolfs and Pastons as the Manors of Caister Pastons and Bardolfs. The best known of the Fastolfs was Sir John who made sufficient money in the Hundred Years War to build Caister Castle. On his death in 1459 the Manors passed to Sir John Paston.[12]

4.   The Parish Church of Holy Trinity, c1875.

Manors conferred on their owners certain beneficial rights, with those on the coast enjoying what was called 'wreck of sea', i.e. the right to anything washed ashore. This was the case at Caister and it was one of the main reasons why the possession of a tract of land, measuring some 400 acres, between the Midsands Cross, in Yarmouth and the southern bank of the Estuary's northern channel, variously called Grub's Haven or Cocklewater, was hotly disputed by the Caister men and those of Yarmouth.[13]

For the purposes of this study the details of this dispute are interesting in respect of the state of the Estuary's northern entrance at the time, and the extent of salvage opportunities created when vessels or goods came ashore.

As early as 1300 Hugh Bardolf made complaint that goods and chattels to the value of £40, belonging to him and other Caister men, had been taken from this land by Yarmouth men. This was probably a reference to cattle, suggesting that at this date it was relatively easy to move livestock across the Cocklewater, a name suggestive of shallowness.

Incidents of this nature occurred at regular intervals thereafter, but in the early 16th century the Bailiffs of Yarmouth made the mistake of not carrying out regular perambulations of the boundaries of this land, thereby encouraging Sir William Paston, lord of the Caister Manors, an eminent lawyer and grandson of Sir John, to seize it. This he did in 1524, but nothing seems to have been done about it until 1544 when the Yarmouth men took the opportunity to complain to the Duke of Norfolk, who at the time was surveying the town's fortifications. He promised to take the matter up with the King and the following year a commission was set up to examine and resolve the dispute.

5. The remains of the Midsands Cross.

6. 'A determined gang of 40 men'. Beachmen outside the Lifeboat Store Shed, c1910.

Back row, left to right; Robert 'Pikey' Sutton, Charles 'Stow' Haylett, John 'Wampo' Brown, Walter Haylett, George 'Wildawn' Green, Bertie 'Geesha' George, George 'Brush' Broom, John 'Sprat' Haylett, Edward 'Ganny' Bullock, Charlie Knights, Walter John Haylett. Middle row; Robert 'Cyreen' Green, John 'Clinker' Brown, Joe 'Jack-in-the-box' Julier. Front row; Jack 'Shell' George, Edwin Haylett, Alfred 'Hansh' Barnard.

Thirteen men gave evidence on behalf of Yarmouth. They claimed that bodies washed ashore on the disputed land had been buried in Yarmouth churchyard, that the Yarmouth gallows had formerly stood there and that Yarmouth men had long grazed cattle on it. They also recalled a number of shipwrecks.

The earliest occurred in 1493, or thereabouts, when Sir John Paston had stood with many people on the north side of the Cocklewater and had addressed around 40 people standing on the Yarmouth side. At the time goods were being washed ashore, 'whiche then and ther wer spoyled and perishid in a shippe of Hulle, freyted with wulle and felle'.[14] He had forbidden the Yarmouth men to cross to gather goods on the Caister side and equally had forbade his own men to cross to the Yarmouth side for the same purpose.

In 1522 the Bailiffs and Chamberlains presented the town with 'four bombs, called guns, whereof two are called slyngs, and the other two called hagbushes, to the value of £10, which the same… received for groundage of a ship belonging to the vice-admiral of Flanders; which said ship was cast away on the sea-shore, by a great wind or tempest, in a certain place called Yarmouth Common…'.[15]

On the 27th February 1524 a determined gang of 40 men, including at least 21 from the two Caister parishes, most of whom were described as husbandmen, 'arrayed in a warlike manner' and armed with 'staves, and knives, pykforkys, brushhokys', carried away two brass guns, an iron gun 'gunnestonys' and other material from a wreck opposite the Midsands Cross.[16]

Furthermore around 1525 'a ship cald an Esterlyng, freyted with wyne and other merchandyse, was brokyn in the Gatt before Yarmouth, and the goodys that wer in hir came on lond in dyvers places, whereof parcell came on lond upon the seid grownde now in variaunce'.[17]

Lastly around 1530 the deponents saw 'a shippe of Breteyn freyted with salt, cald the Julyan lyeng on grounde bethewyn the seid Grubby's Havyn and the seid Ston Cros… whiche shippe by violens of the see was there throwne upon the shoore and soore brosed and broken on the botom, and all the salt was washen out into the see…'[18]

On the 30th April 1546, having heard the depositions and examined the site, the commissioners made known their decision. Unable to choose between the two parties they divided the land between them. A ditch 12 feet wide was dug and rails set up equidistant between the Midsands Cross and the Cocklewater, a line that still forms the boundary between Caister and Yarmouth today.[19]

Writing in the early 17th century Henry Manship, the Yarmouth historian, had great difficulty locating the site of the Cocklewater stating that, 'no remain of any Haven is there to be seen: for, in the year of our Lord, 1578, at such time as Queen Elizabeth came to Norwich, and many lords of Her Majesty's Council to Yarmouth, the same, by commandment of Sir William Paston, for more easy passage, was levelled and made even with the common, aforesaid'.[20]

With the disappearance of Caister's southern shoreline such seafaring activity as there was in the village became concentrated on the more exposed eastern coast and over the years the village was drawn in this direction, along what was to become Beach Road. Not that this activity amounted to much, comprising little more than 'wreck of sea' and 'longshore fishing.

In 1565, with Britain at war with Spain, a survey of boats and sailors was taken, but Caister does not appear in the list.[21] A hundred years later, in 1664, on the eve of the first Anglo-Dutch war, another survey of seamen was carried out and this time 17 men were listed for Caister, two of whom were described as 'Imprestmen now in service'. These were the youngest, Robert Reeder

7. 'Which said ship was cast away on the sea-shore'. The Motor-schooner Moorside ashore at Caister in April 1919. She was broken up where she lay.

8. Drawnet fishing from Caister Beach, c1950. This simple form of fishing was timeless. The men hauling the net are Walter Haylett's sons Herbert, Alfred and Robert. The boat is Herbert's *Silver Quest*, YH 658.

and John Baker, both aged 20.[22] This does not suggest a large seafaring population and it was not until the closing years of the 18th century that the Caister men took to the sea in earnest.

There was, however, another activity at Caister, which related directly to seafaring in these early years and that was navigational lighting. The coast off Caister was treacherous and sailors needed all the help they could get to avoid disaster. The introduction of shore-based lights was therefore welcomed, offering some measure of assistance, particularly at night and in bad weather.

As early as 1282 a beacon was kept alight at Caister, with the masters of customable vessels paying two pence 'fire-pence' by way of a toll.[23] Towards the close of the 16th century, in response to the growth in the coal trade, Thomas Bushell erected two wooden lighthouses at the northern end of the village, lit by candle light. In 1600, under pressure to erect lights at Winterton, the Trinity Brethren surveyed the Yarmouth Roads and came to the conclusion that Caister was the best location and promptly purchased Bushell's structures, paying him a salary to maintain them.

In 1628, a Mr Hill became the lightkeeper and was paid £37 per annum, provided he 'live at Castor; in either lighthouse to have three candles of three to the pound; light all the candles immediately after sunset and continue them burning until fair day'.[24] Ignoring the spirit of this condition Hill employed a woman who lived some miles from the village, to carry out his duties, but complaint was made, for in bad weather she stayed at home, leaving the lights unlit. In similar vein, in 1663 it was considered that a vessel was lost off Caister because the lights were not lit and as a result the keeper was dismissed.

Mention is made of these lights throughout the 18th century and the parish register records the burial, on the 19th December 1766, of James Howes, a married man 'from Caister Light House'.

Faden's map of 1797 shows two lights blazing away, but they were taken down in the early 19th century, their role passing to lighthouses further north. They stood on land now beneath the waves at the end of Second Avenue.

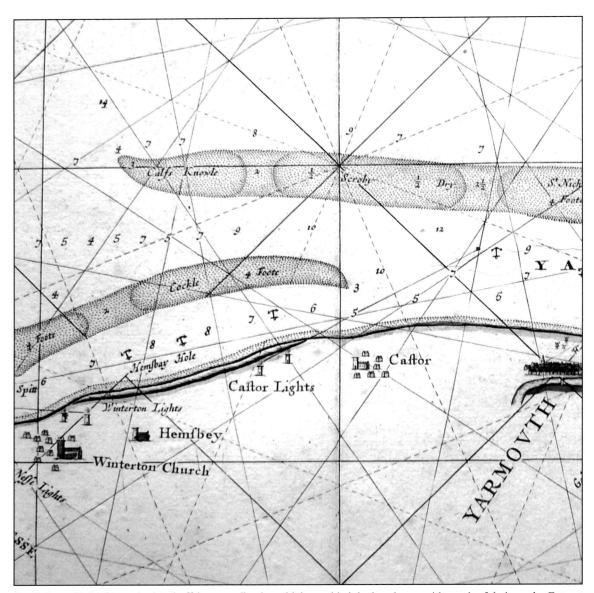

9. Caister, the Lights and related offshore sandbanks, which provided the beachmen with much of their work. Extract from a chart published by Captain Greenville Collins as part of his Coasting Pilot, in 1693.

2. 1790 – 1815

During the 18th century Great Britain emerged as the world's first industrial nation, a transformation that prompted a dramatic rise in the number of vessels plying their trade along the East Coast. This gave rise to the formation of organisations called beach companies, groups of 'longshore fishermen who banded together to service shipping and more importantly reap the benefits of offshore salvage.[25]

The reason this work existed was the paradoxical nature of the Roadstead off Yarmouth and Lowestoft. The coast of East Anglia is 'soft', enabling the sea to easily reshape it. For centuries its clay cliffs have been eroded, with the material taken being deposited further south as beach, offshore sand banks, or, in the case of the site of Yarmouth, both. In this way a crescent of sandbanks was created in front of the two towns, a barrier which by breaking the force of the sea, produced the only relatively safe anchorage between Tyne and Thames. But in bad weather entering or leaving the Roads was a hazardous business and even if anchored within, the unmanageable nature of sailing ships in such conditions meant they often had to cut and run before the wind. In these circumstances collisions were commonplace and worse, vessels would be driven onto the sandbanks or the shore, providing ample work for the ever-vigilant beachmen.

Salvage was a lucrative business and rights to benefit from it had in early times been granted to the lords of coastal manors, but the sandbank system off Yarmouth was special and in 1559 Elizabeth I granted the town an Admiralty Court which enabled the burgesses to control all offshore

10. The Tolhouse at Great Yarmouth, c1890. The Admiralty Court sat in the upper chamber. Below ground are the cells in which such men as Daniel Green, William Davey and Edward Bullock were incarcerated until they paid their fines.

salvage activity, from Winterton Ness to Eastern Ness, and make a great deal of money in the process. There was, of course, no love lost between the Court and the beachmen, but each needed the other.[26]

By the early 18th century beach companies were to be found in the coastal towns and by mid-century the villages too. The period of the French Wars accelerated their development, but all was not plain sailing, for Yarmouth became an important naval base and with the Navy came competition for salvage and the iniquitous press gang to add to the interference already meted out by the men of the revenue cruisers in their daily search for smugglers. It is against this backdrop that the origins and early days of the Caister Beach Company are set.

The precise date a beach company was formed at Caister will probably never be known, but the available evidence points to the mid-1780s. Prior to 1785 the entries for salvaged goods in the Admiralty Court's registers were not plentiful, but from then there was a marked rise, due either to an increase in goods salvaged or, what seems more likely, the Court taking positive steps to enforce its rights. Whatever the reason it is thereafter possible to pick out the salvaging activities of an interrelated group of Caister men.

Between 1787 and 1794 William Brooks was the sole Sea Reeve at Caister, the officer responsible for ensuring that salvaged goods were declared to the Admiralty Court. He himself entered goods between 1789 and 1791 and it was the practice of the Court to appoint prominent salvagers to these positions.

At the same time Caister men James and Samuel Stagg were also entering goods. From at least 1789 until 1792 James was the publican of an inn called the King's Head and Samuel followed

11. The Lord Nelson Tavern, Beach Road, 1975. It was the successor to the King's Head and the Lord Duncan. The inquest into the 1901 disaster deaths was held here.

12. Landing the Wounded at Yarmouth after the Battle of Camperdown, 1797. Print by Rowlandson. It shows six captured Dutch ships of the line, including the flagship *Vreiheid,* the bowsprit from which was salvaged by the Caister beachmen led by John Smith.

him in that role until 1795. When James died that year he mentions in his will his son-in-law William Brooks and describes him as a mariner.

A third strand is provided by Benjamin Ellis. He entered goods in 1786 and between 1794 and 1798 was a Sea Reeve in Yarmouth. He became the Sea Reeve for Caister in 1799, the same year he is listed as the publican of the Lord Duncan. The other Caister inn licensed throughout this period was the Kings Arms, the predecessor of the present day public house of that name. It would seem that the King's Head became the Lord Duncan in 1799 and after 1805 the Lord Nelson, the name changes reflecting progress in the naval war and the inn's proximity to the sea, it being in Beach Road. It is probable that these men were the leading lights in a small Beach Company mustering 10-15 men, sufficient to launch and man a single yawl.

Things become clearer in the next decade with a piece of salvage work linking the Caister men to national events. On the 11th October, 1797, Admiral Duncan defeated the Dutch at the Battle of Camperdown and brought the captured prizes back to his naval base in the Yarmouth Roads. The *Vrieheid*, the flagship of the Dutch admiral, de Winter, was one of them and while in the Roads 38 feet of her bowsprit, together with a 32lb shot lodged within it, was cut away. This was retrieved abreast Paines Gibbet, between Yarmouth and Caister, by a Caister crew under John Smith and salvage was duly paid.

The only major salvage case for the Caister beachmen in this period occurred in 1801. On the 28th November that year the brigantine *Aberdeen Merchant* of Sunderland set sail from Hull for London with a cargo of potatoes. The voyage started well and by late afternoon the following day the master, Eustace Barrett, was pleased to be entering Yarmouth Roads. It was then that disaster struck as, without warning, his vessel suddenly grounded on the Outer Barber Sand, off Caister.

Barrett got both pumps working, but after half an hour found that the water in the vessel's hold was gaining fast, and with the sea breaking freely over her decks he decided it was time to take to the ship's boat. Over two hours later he and his exhausted crew managed to make landfall at Yarmouth. To the delight of the Caister beachmen the brigantine survived the night and, led by John Bickers and Henry Swartley, they boarded her and, after effecting repairs, set sail and anchored her in the Roads. As she was a derelict, i.e. having no living person on board, they were rewarded with a handsome £200.

The following year the Caister men were not so fortunate when they had to bow to the superiority of their northern neighbours at Winterton. On the 5th November the ship *Betsey* sailed from Cronstadt, in Russia, for London with a general cargo. After a two week voyage, in the darkness of early morning, she struck what proved to be the Haisborough Sand. Thomas Ridley, her master, tried hard to extricate his ship, but at daybreak he was forced to hoist a distress signal. Water was filling her hold and eventually, with no obvious sign of help on the way, he gave the order to abandon ship.

While this was happening there was a flurry of excitement on the shore. Beachmen on lookout at Winterton, Happisburgh and Caister spotted the casualty and the race was on to secure what would prove to be a valuable prize. At Caister John Bickers gathered together a crew of twelve and

13. The *Betsey*, coming through the Cockle Gat, with a cod smack providing the steering. Drawing by Roger Finch. The Caister men lost out on what proved to be a very lucrative salvage job.

with Trinity pilot David Burwood aboard, set off. Unfortunately for them, they arrived at the *Betsey* shortly after the last Winterton boat. There was an unwritten rule amongst the various companies that the first boat to reach a casualty secured the job. Ignoring this the Caister men tried to board, but as the ship was still stuck on the sandbank they were resisted with handspikes and boathooks and a brief yet furious fight ensued. Eventually they were forced to withdraw after Burwood's offer of pilotage services was refused.

They continued to stand by while the ship was extricated, but eventually had to return home unrewarded, having paid the price for failing to get to the *Betsey* first. Nevertheless they put in a claim for services rendered, but the Admiralty Court judge decided that they had not been necessary in the case and gave them nothing, whereas the Winterton men eventually received £40 per man.[27]

With the resumption of the war in 1803 seamen were once more obliged to apply for exemption from impressment into the Navy and an entry in the registers for this essential requirement reveals the name of a Caister yawl, the *Assistance*. Reference is made to a crew of eight with John Bickers as master of the 17-ton boat. He and his crew were granted exemption by virtue of their work in 'Assisting ships in distress, carrying off pilots and at the Yarmouth Ferry'.[28]

The fact that they were bracketed with three Yarmouth yawls is instructive. The later company was almost exclusively a salvage affair with passenger ferrying and shipping pilots a very small part of their income. It may well be, though, that at this time these other aspects were more significant, especially as the leading man at the time, John Bickers, was a Trinity pilot. With the Winterton Company better placed to secure the salvage work to the north of Caister it is possible that the Caister beachmen concentrated on servicing shipping in the Roads, working in effect as another Yarmouth company. What is clear from the Admiralty Court records is that entries of salvaged goods by Caister men are not noteworthy until 1809.

There is, however, another explanation for this shortage of entries. On the 31st May 1803 John Bickers, John Trunham, Henry Key, George Horth, Henry Swartley and William Hunn were found guilty and fined 10 guineas for selling an anchor without entering it into the Court. Similarly on the 20th August 1811 Daniel Green, William Davey and Edward Bullock, 'all of Caister, boatmen', were tried for landing two anchors and two pieces of cable and later another anchor, all of which they did not enter into the Court. Each was fined 10 guineas and threatened with gaol unless they paid. Refusing to pay they were locked up until the 27th August when they finally bowed to the inevitable.

It can be imagined that trying to avoid the involvement of the Admiralty Court was something the beachmen did as a matter of course, if they thought they could get away with it. Many illegal deals must have been struck between beachmen and master. This must always be remembered when drawing conclusions from the court records.

In 1803 the Company launched to the *Hannah* of London, offering advice and assistance to her master, Thomas Sidsworth. Not satisfied with what he was prepared to pay the case came before the Admiralty Court and the Caister men were awarded 30 guineas. Mention was made of John Bickers, Henry Swartley and John Smith.

The last case to highlight in this period shows that not only did the Caister men have to play second fiddle to those at Winterton, but also to the Yarmouth beachmen to the south. On the 25th November 1812 the brigantine *Susanna* sailed from London for Hartley, with ashes onboard as ballast. Two days later, she struck the Scroby Sand. Her master, Roger Sanderson, ordered a distress signal to be hoisted, but after two hours, with there being no help forthcoming, he and his crew abandoned the vessel and rowed to Caister for assistance. It took another two and a half hours before a Caister yawl took them back to the brigantine, only to find that she was in the possession of James Boult and his company of Yarmouth beachmen. Boult refused to allow the crew or the Caister men to board. After getting her into Yarmouth harbour Boult entered her in the Admiralty Court and received £225 for his company's efforts. Once more the Caister men had paid the price for not getting to a casualty quickly enough.

The impression gained is that the Caister Beach Company at this time was not as experienced or vigorous as its competitors and therefore had to rely on servicing and low key salvage work. It was only when, on the rare occasion, a major casualty landed on its doorstep that a good payment was forthcoming. The reason for this seems to be its small size and the fact that not all its members were seamen.

Those that were, were conscious of the ever-present threat of the press gang as the Navy had an insatiable appetite for experienced seamen. In general terms fishermen were free from impressment because fishing was important to feeding the nation. Before the start of a voyage the master of a fishing boat would apply for a certificate of exemption for him and his crew. This would keep them safe at sea, but they could still be taken on land.

Fearing invasion, the Government raised, among other units, a coastal home guard called Sea Fencibles. Carried away with enthusiasm the naval officers in charge raised as many men as they could from the fishing communities, there being no lack of willing recruits as enlistment provided exemption from impressment.

Between 1803 and 1810 a small number of Caister men served as Sea Fencibles, but unlike at Winterton where there was a separate unit of over 60 men, they were part of the Yarmouth establishment, reinforcing the view that at this time, for nautical purpose, Caister was seen as part of Yarmouth. Not being separately listed they have to be picked out from the pay lists, for Yarmouth, but the familiar names of John Bickers, Daniel Green, George Horth, William Hunn, Henry Key, John Smith, Henry Swartley and John Trunham are there, the men who formed the nucleus of the Beach Company at this time.[29]

All enlisted in July 1803 except Daniel Green who waited until December, but only Hunn and Green served through to 1810, none of the others doing so beyond February 1804. Service as a Sea Fencible was not very onerous there being only a nominal requirement to exercise for no more than four times a month until 1805 and one day thereafter. Even then their normal seafaring work, took precedence.

Of the company individuals known from this period John Bickers was a Sea Reeve in 1802 and was the leading man until drowned in November 1808 when returning from Harwich, having taken a vessel there. He had been a pilot for 14 years and before that a master mariner. Henry Swartley was also a Sea Reeve, in 1802. Daniel Green was a prominent property owner with interests in Beach Road and William Davey was from the family, which later ran the East Mill, also in Beach Road. Three other names can be added to the list, Joseph Saunders, Thomas London, a Sea Reeve from 1801 to 1806 and again in 1809, and lastly John George. George was a Winterton fisherman/beachman who married in Caister in 1813. He represents the beginning of the migration of experienced Winterton seafarers to Caister.

No survey of beach activity would be complete without reference to smuggling, although there is little evidence that Caister men took part in the illegal trade at this time (nor should there be if they were successful). The Customs service, however, was aware of the possibilities, and from as early as 1684 men termed riding officers were appointed to watch the coast, with the one stationed at Caister patrolling from the Caister Lights to the Yarmouth Haven.

14. 'Longshore fishing boats on Caister beach, c1900. The Manor House hotel stands above the dunes and fishing
smacks can to be seen on the horizon.

To avoid fraternisation it was usual to appoint outsiders to these positions, but when James
Colby died in 1803 Caister man William Everitt was appointed to replace him. Seemingly not
everyone's choice he soon found himself the subject of an anonymous letter written to the customs
officers by someone calling himself 'A Friend to the Revenue'. It was alleged that Everitt had
accepted the office of Fen Reeve from the Lord of the Manor thereby serving two masters and that
he was busily impounding horses that had strayed on to Caister Common, charging up to 2s.6d.
per head to release them. In effect he was accused of being a precursor of the modern day car
clamper. It was also claimed that in order to avoid retaliation he did not keep a horse of his own,
making it difficult for him to carry out his duties.[30]

Furthermore it was said that he falsified his journals, claiming to have carried out patrols that
had not taken place. Finally it was stated that 'There is little occasion for an officer of this
description at Caister as they never made a seisure there these 20 years and have so much idle time
they are burthensome to themselves and a nuisance to the public'.[31]

The matter was investigated, but without the informant being able to be identified, the customs
officers accepted Everitt's rebuttal, which included the fact that his mare was in foal and therefore
he was using one belonging to his brother. By May 1804 Everitt was riding his own horse again.
Returning from patrol one day he turned her out onto the Common to feed but later found she had
been 'driven into or unfortunately walked into the sea during the heat of the day and was
drowned'.[32] Everitt discovered her 30 yards from the shore, but despite hiring a boat he could not
save her.

Everitt clearly suspected foul play, but little more is heard of him until his death in post in 1809.
The last riding officer at Caister was William Waite, who arrived by boat with his family, from
Anderby, in Lincolnshire, in January 1823.

The basic work of most beachmen was 'longshore fishing. It is difficult to know how many
'longshore boats there were on Caister beach at this time, but as a measure to control smuggling,

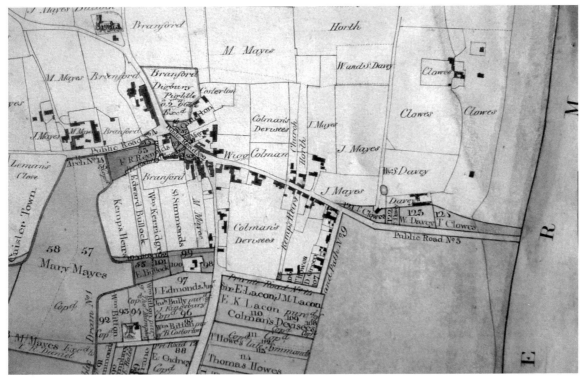

15. Caister in 1813. Extract from the Inclosure Map.

vessels of a certain size had to be licensed by the Admiralty on the recommendation of the local customs officers. One Caister boat is mentioned in the records, the open lugger *Industry*, owned and skippered by William Hunn, but it can be assumed there were several others.

Throughout this period there was an active mackerel and herring fishery run from Yarmouth, but the Caister men do not seem to have played a significant part in it. Few, if any, skippered the Yarmouth luggers, but they no doubt made up part of the crews.

Turning to the village and its people the first national population census was taken in 1801. This revealed that there were 498 people at Caister, making it the second most populous parish on Flegg after Martham. These people comprised 106 families, living in 102 houses.

By 1811 the population had risen to 629 with 136 families occupying 132 houses, but in both census' what was described as Caister was the parish, which included several groups of houses in West Caister. Occupational data is included, but it is impossible to distinguish the small number of seafarers from the rest of the population, which was strongly agricultural in character.

The Inclosure Map of 1813 gives the first detailed picture of the village.[33] It shows it as having a linear form, focused on what is now the High Street, between its junction with West Road and the turn off to Beach Road. From there the houses are spread out along the south side of Beach Road, as far as the junction with what is now Victoria Street and along the west side of that street.

The church is isolated from the village, a distance which in people terms was actually greater as the nearest buildings to it were malthouses. Beach Road is the main street, a conclusion reinforced by the fact that on the plan of 1802, mentioned below, it is called 'Caister Street'. There is little development on the southern part of the current High Street, which was extremely narrow, with a pinchpoint at the northern end. It is clear that the village had been drawn towards the beach, rather than the crossing to Yarmouth.

Tan Lane and Victoria Street are depicted as wide, straight roads, forming a right angle between Beach Road and the High Street. This represents a road improvement carried out by the Inclosure Commissioners, the more irregular, earlier form being shown on Faden's Map of 1797. The Victoria Street section was the start of the beach village. It is probably here that several of the seafarers lived at this time.

With one or two exceptions the dwellings were simple, single storey, cottages built of beach flints, or brick, with steeply pitched thatched roofs, sporting dormer windows. The beach flints and reed thatch were local materials and the bricks were mostly made in the village. There was also another 'local material' and that was ships timbers, salvaged from the vessels wrecked on the beach. These were extensively recycled and may well survive today in the roofs of the older properties.

Moving down to the beach, the available evidence does not confirm that there were structures there, other than the lighthouses north of the village, but it is to be presumed that the Beach Company had some form of watch-house and lookout.

Close to the beach, to the north of the gap, stood the Manor House, a location which helped foster the interest the Lords of the Manors took in the Caister seafarers. At the start of this period Sir John Rous, baronet, was in possession, but by December 1791 he had sold them to Major Henry Alexander. It was Alexander who rebuilt the Manor House, between 1791 and 1793, at a cost of £2,600, the half million bricks needed being made on site by Thomas Plane.

In 1803 Alexander sold the manors to Thomas Clowes, thereby starting the close relationship this family had with the village for over a century. There was, however, a sad postscript to the Major's involvement with local seafaring for in 1806 his eldest son, Hector, fell to his death from

16. The Manor House, c1910, as built by Major Henry Alexander between 1791 and 1793, at a cost of £2,600.

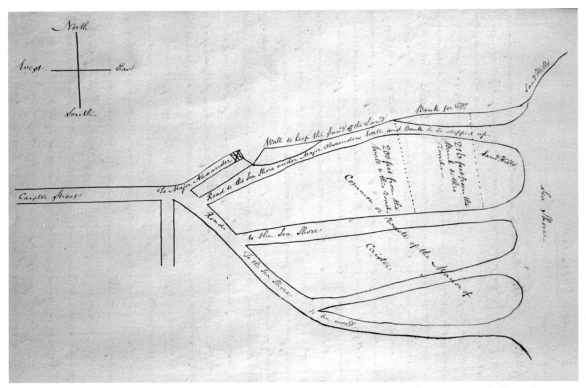

17. Road Closure Order Plan of 1802 showing four public routes to the beach, from the northern end of what is now Victoria Street. By 1813 these had been reduced to one, the present day Beach Road.

the rigging of *H.M.S Resolution*, while she was anchored in the Yarmouth Roads.

An interesting insight into how access was gained to the beach at Caister is shown by the plan, which accompanied a road closure order of 1802.[34] There were, at that time, four tracks branching out from the end of Victoria Street across Caister Common. The order closed to the public the northern most one, which was on the line of Old Mill Road. By 1813 two of the others were no longer considered to be public roads, leaving the one in use today.

3. 1815-1865

Victory over the French at Waterloo was followed by a period of social and economic uncertainty, but this did not discourage the Caister beachmen for in 1816 they invested in a new yawl, the *Prince Blucher*, a 15 ton, Yarmouth built boat, some 44 feet long. The choice of name is a little bizarre, for while other beach companies were honouring English heroes, such as Nelson and Wellington, the Caister men chose to commemorate the role played by a Prussian general in Bonaparte's defeat.

Shortly after the arrival of this boat, with salvage work increasing, the Beach Company embarked on a period of expansion, which, by the 1840s had resulted in the membership being fixed at 40, prompting the shipowners to dub the company 'the Forty Thieves'.

The details of this transformation would not have been so clear were it not for the fact that the beachmen tended to commit their transactions to paper, a convention which owed much to the influence of the Clowes family, who practised law in nearby Yarmouth.

It is not known how many men initially shared the ownership of the *Prince Blucher*, but when she was re-registered in 1825 there were 18 of them. In 1829 the Company took possession of the 17-ton yawl *Storm*, built by Francis Holmes at Southtown. Being only 35 feet 11 inches long she was shorter, but heavier, than the *Prince Blucher* and as her name implies she was designed to venture out when the weather was too severe to risk the lighter, faster yawls. She was in effect the Company's lifeboat.

The *Storm* was registered to 31 men and while these included the *Prince Blucher* owners, or their successors, there had clearly been a significant increase in company membership. Writing in 1836 William White confirmed that at Caister there were 30 beachmen. [35]

By 1832 the Company had acquired a number of other beach craft to carry out their salvage work. That year John Smith sold his share to John Winson (the Caister pronunciation of Vincent) for 13 guineas and the transfer document lists the yawls *Prince Blucher*, *Storm*, *Venus*, *Edward*

18. 'Caister from the Beach', 1822. Engraving by Joseph Lambert.

and *Industry*, together with the coble *Star* and the gig *Pernicity*.

Details of some of the Company's activities at this time are provided by the Yarmouth Admiralty Court records. Between 1815 and the close of the Court in 1835 Thomas London, William Hunn and Henry Key were the principal men entering goods salvaged on the beach or the sandbanks off Caister, i.e. the Barber, the Patch and Scroby. Daniel Green was the Court's Caister Sea Reeve between 1822 and 1827 and he was followed by another company man, John George.

In 1825 William Green and John Saunders were caught playing the old trick of not declaring salvaged goods. Each was fined 20s. and as usual, were placed in gaol until the fine was paid. In June 1828 the Court pronounced on a claim by Thomas London and the Company for services rendered to the *Black Joke*. Having been stranded on Caister beach this Yarmouth fishing lugger had been extricated and taken into Yarmouth Harbour. For services rendered the Caister men received £40.

The highlight of these decades was the salvage of the sloop *Bee*, of Kincardine. In April 1831, under her master, Henry Anderson, she had sailed from Largo, with a cargo of potatoes, bound for London. Having moored off Winterton to await the tide she had set off, in thick fog, for the Cockle Gat. Missing the buoy, and finding his vessel in five fathoms of water, Anderson let go the small bower anchor. As the tide dropped so the sloop struck the ground and with two feet of water in her hold he and his crew took to the sloop's boat. After sheltering on a brig for a while, they eventually summoned up enough courage to venture back to the sloop only to find she now had six feet of water in her hold. An hour later they left again, this time for Yarmouth, but on the way they fell in with a gig crewed by William Hunn, Henry Key, Robert Howes and three others. These Caister beachmen refused to take them back to the sloop, and after pumping her out they took her into the Roads, by which time Anderson had managed to get back on board. The case was contested in the

19. 'Yarmouth Beach and Jetty in 1846'. Lithograph by J. M. Johnson, after a painting by William Joy. This was part of the environment within which the Caister men operated.

20. 'Veering Down to Wreck', from a drawing by C.J. Staniland, 1885. This engraving gives the flavour of what it was like to head for a casualty on the sandbanks, whether by yawl or lifeboat.

Admiralty Court in the usual way, but eventually the Caister men were awarded £108.15s.1d. less tax.

Thus far the Beach Company was very much a local affair, with the shareholders drawn from Caister men. In the 1820s and 1830s the predominant surnames were Blyth, Bullock, Church, Davey, Green, Horth, Howes, Hunn, Key, Knowles, Nichols, Nicklin, Purdy, Read, Simmonds, Smith, Sutton, Thompson, Trunham, Vincent and Woodhouse.

This was all about to change as many of their old rivals from Winterton decided to settle in the village. New surnames became prominent, Barnard, Brown, Dyble, George, Haylett, Hodds, Kettle, King and Plummer, names that would come to personify the Caister 'Never Turn Back' spirit.

Migration from Winterton had its roots in rapid population growth and the expansion of the Yarmouth fishing industry. Yarmouth was the obvious attraction, it seeming senseless to many to keep making the 18 mile round trip to and from the port, but for those who wanted to retain a village way of life Caister was the nearest place to be.

It is difficult to know if John or Robert George migrated first. John probably arrived around 1810, before marrying in the village in 1813. Robert, not a close relative, made the move between 1810 and 1812, bringing with him his wife, Elizabeth, and a young child. In 1815 he had a house built, in what would become Victoria Street, which still bears the date and his initials. It is now The Ship Inn. Both these men had shares in the *Prince Blucher*.

Their example encouraged other Winterton men to settle in Caister, namely, Samuel George and

21. Beachmen posing outside the Company watch-house, c1870. The impact of the Winterton migration is clearly evident as seven of the eleven men are of Winterton origin.

Front row, seated, left to right; William Knowles, William Read, John Vincent, Philip George (with chart). Standing, Robert Read (holding telescope), Aaron Haylett (holding gong). On the stairs, bottom to top; Isaiah Haylett (stovepipe hat), Aaron King, 'Matches' Hodds, John Haylett. On the staging Joe Haylett (looking through telescope).

Edward George before 1820; Thomas George between 1820 and 1830; William George, Benjamin Hodds and John Haylett between 1820 and 1840, and William Hodds, John Plummer and Humphrey Dyble between 1840 and 1850. Many of these men brought their families with them to swell the population of the fast growing beach village.

The superior seafaring qualities and experience these men possessed quickly established them as a ruling elite in the Caister Beach Company. On the 24th February 1848, 32 of the 40 members attended a meeting in the Company watch-house to finalise the rules by which they should operate. Of these nearly half were of Winterton stock, including six out of the seven-man committee, which had formulated the rules under the chairmanship of Benjamin Hodds. The only Caister man on the committee was Samuel Simmonds.

The next decade was to witness a further influx of Winterton men, who all but took over the company. These included Isaiah Haylett, Aaron King, Robert King, Benjamin Kettle, Jacob George, Philip George, John George and the most famous of them all, Jimmy Haylett, who arrived in 1850 and bought a share in the Company from Thomas Horth in 1852. The 1841 census reveals some 30 people related to Winterton born heads of households in Caister. By 1851 this figure had risen to 60 and by 1861, to 88.

Ironically this process was accelerated by a tragedy, which occurred on the 14th June 1847. A Caister yawl with seven men aboard took an anchor to Yarmouth. Having delivered it three of them decided to walk home, leaving the other four to sail back in the yawl. Unfortunately while running down near the Caister Rails the boat upset. Spotting the disaster the Caister men immediately launched a rescue boat only to find, on arrival, that the yawl was bottom upwards. Winterton born John Haylett, swam ashore, but Caister men Robert Howes (57), Samuel Key, (57), and James Church (47), were all drowned. The deceased were described as elderly men.

Beach Companies, like any other operational group, needed rules or a code of practice to regulate their affairs. In the early days the rules were simple, but as company organisation and work became more complex, so the rules were elaborated to ensure the continued harmony so necessary for success. A Beach Company was essentially a team and the best rewards came to those teams able to act quickly through being disciplined and well organised. Company rules were formulated to ensure that each member made maximum effort to be in the first boat to go off, that communal property was well maintained, and that those injured or killed and their dependants, were well looked after.

The rules agreed in 1848 were printed and were revised at least five times, in 1849, 1862 1888, 1907 and 1936. The preamble to the first set encapsulates the nature of the Company, 'THE

22. 'The Look-out', from a drawing by C.J. Staniland, 1885. The Company telescopes are now on display in the Lifeboat Visitor Centre.

23. Beach boats and lifeboats, Caister beach c1895. The boat in the foreground is the gig *Ubique*. Behind her are the lifeboats *Beauchamp* and *Covent Garden*.

CAISTER COMPANY OF BEACHMEN, formed for the purpose of saving property, and of rendering assistance to vessels or ships aground, stranded, or wrecked on the sands or beach, or in any kind of difficulty, distress, or disaster at sea, consists of forty Shareholders, having an equal share, right, and interest in certain boats, boat-house or shed, tackling, etc. lying and being in the parish of Caister, next Yarmouth, in the county of Norfolk.

The remuneration, earnings, and emoluments, arising from any such services, shall be divided and apportioned in certain Shares for the maintenance of the Boats belonging to the Company, and amongst those Members of the Company, who shall be entitled to share in any such earnings, under and according to the following RULES AND REGULATIONS'.[36]

There follows nine basic rules; I. How entitled to share, II. In what proportion, III. Leaving the beach, IV. Night-watch, V. Hurt or injury, VI. Death, VII. Widow or nearest relation, VIII. New members and IX. Chairman to be chosen.

In essence the company existed to make money from saving both property and life in relation to vessels in difficulties in and around the sandbanks off Caister. The inclusion of life in this definition may seem surprising to a readership familiar with the beachmen as heroic lifeboatmen, but, while heroes they undoubtedly were, it must always be remembered that they went to sea to earn a living and in this context a reward for saving life was expected. This was understood by those providing lifeboats. That is why they gave rewards as incentives to launch. As will be seen a usable lifeboat became operational at Caister in 1846, and when the rules were formalised two years later mention is made of money earned when it was used. Case 9 under Rule II. states that, 'When the Life-Boat is used by the Company, all, who shall go off in her, shall receive ten shillings each out of any sum or sums, if sufficient, awarded or obtained as a remuneration for saving lives…'.

The beachmen were essentially nautical Jacks-of-all-trades, turning their hands to anything, which might offer a reward for their efforts. Much of their work was of a speculative nature, requiring a hunter's instinct and a great deal of effort to achieve a worthwhile result. Often enough the work was extremely dull and arduous, with little recompense for the patience and determination that was expended.

The simple entries in the Beach Company account books chart the largely mundane nature of the Caister beachmen's work.[37] Between 1842 and 1865 the income section reveals 372 entries relating to services to shipping, 85 involving the retrieval of anchors in the Roads (termed swiping), a further 29 for salvaging the buoys and ropes, which had been attached to the anchors, 65 entries for taking out shipping agents, 12 for shipping passengers, and 4 relating to taking out pilots. A further 272 entries related to the sale of materials including 'rucker', 'paper stuff' and 'raffle', with rucker being rope which was sold as such, paper stuff being old rope, which was sent away to be made into paper, and raffle being general wreckage. In addition 73 entries were made for the sale of wreckage. Between 1845 and 1856 there were also some 64 entries 'for mackerel', mostly in May and June, the mackerel fishing season, when company boats were used for this purpose.

The work that most excited the newspaper reporters was the direct involvement with vessels, because this often produced drama, either at sea or in the courtroom. In December 1838 the *Adventure* of Newcastle, mistaking the Newarp light for that at Winterton in thick fog, struck the Cross Sand. After taking steps to ensure that the vessel got no further onto the Sand the master hoisted a light, prompting two yawls to launch from Caister. On arrival the beachmen laid a kedge

24. Beachmen playing cards in the Company watch-house, 1934. By then the Company was more like a social club than an active salvage organisation.

Working round the table from the bottom left; Charlie Lacock, Walter 'Sequah' Haylett, Nat Brown, Charlie 'Munch' Barnard, Charlie Knights, Oliver 'Bones' Hodds, Solly Brown, Jack Plummer, 'Flow' Westgate Saunders, Joe Woodhouse and Harry 'Prince' Green.

25. California, c1895, from a watercolour by Stephen Batchelder. After 1850 the California Beach Company was Caister's main rival. The picture shows the Company watch-house, lookout and yawls. That part of California south of the Cart Gap, was in the parish of Caister. Several California men eventually settled in Caister.

anchor and at ebb tide moved it to pull in a different direction, but without good effect. Later the master went ashore and secured the services of 14 coal heavers and when they had lightened the cargo the vessel was refloated.

Six years later, in November 1844, the schooner *Cinderella* struck the Sheringham Shoals in heavy squalls, at night. She was discovered at daybreak off the Newarp Sand, flying a distress signal. At the subsequent Adjudication hearing at Yarmouth, John Brett with the crew of the fishing lugger *Saucy Jack* and Robert George and the Caister Beach Company were awarded £300 for their services. Interestingly, John Brett, although fishing for herring out of Yarmouth at the time, was also a member of the Beach Company and probably ensured that the Caister men were employed, rather than any other company. As usual the Clowes family represented the salvors at the hearing.

Not all salvage cases were heard locally and in April 1851 the Caister men found themselves telling the tale in London. On the 30th November the previous year the brig *Elizabeth Young*, while proceeding from London to Shields in ballast, got stuck on the Barber Sand and the master hoisted a distress signal. The *Zephyr*, with a crew of 11, went off followed by the *Star*. Anchors were laid and the vessel was salvaged. The brig was valued at £1,000. The Caister men had offered to do the work for £80, but the master had unwisely opted to let the matter be settled in court, for the award was £120. Of this £6.9s.10d. was entered in the accounts 'for the boat', i.e. for Company property maintenance, the remainder being doled out to the beachmen who had been directly involved.

Until 1841 the Company was only in competition with those at Winterton and Yarmouth, but that year a small Winterton led colony was established at Newport and around 1850 another was set up at California. Both produced beach companies, but it was the one at California, which posed the bigger threat, and, such was the early rivalry that in April 1856 a case of assault was heard at the County Magistrates Court. Henry Brown of California claimed that he and six others had gone off to a vessel in the Cockle Gat and that the Caister men had arrived about the same time. Neither were employed, but when Brown was clambering aboard, Jacob George, one of the Caister men, had 'caught him by the throat and struck him violently endeavouring to break his hold away and threatening to throw him into the sea'. The Court acknowledged that the Caister men had arrived first and that the assault 'arose out of the jealously of rival beach companies'.[38] Notwithstanding this George and his fellow defendant, William Read, were each fined 30s and ordered to pay all costs.

Despite their rivalry these companies would often enough work together when the need arose. In May 1857 the brig *Amelia*, of and from Hartlepool for London, with coal was extricated from the Scroby Sand by beachmen from Caister and Newport, the companies sharing £195 for their efforts.

The same month the *Young John*, bound for Yarmouth, from Sunderland, with coal, earthenware and sacks, got stranded on the Outer Barber, at night. Spotting torchlight Thomas George, Benjamin Kettle and 13 others launched the yawl *Zephyr*. After pulling with great difficulty for about an hour they found the vessel and were at once employed. Setting a kedge anchor, they heaved on a windless, worked the pumps, and got her off. At daybreak they took her into the harbour. For this the Adjudication Court awarded a cursory £35 to which the salvors 'loudly expressed their dissatisfaction'.

In September 1860 there was an Adjudication hearing in Yarmouth, which demonstrated how

26. 'The Caister men decided to work with the tugs rather than oppose them'. A paddle tug is seen carrying out its normal towage work, c 1890. YH217 is the trawling smack *Glance*.

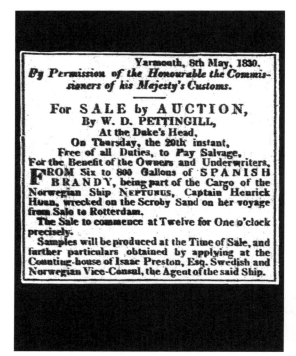

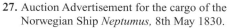

27. Auction Advertisement for the cargo of the Norwegian Ship *Neptumus,* 8th May 1830.

28. 'The Face of a Beachman'. Charlie Lacock, coxswain of the lifeboat 1919-1935.

the steam tug had come to challenge the 'rights' of the beachmen to all salvage work. On the 28th August the Caister men observed a vessel anchored south-west of the Barber Sand, with both pumps working. She turned out to be the brig *Waterloo*, of Cley, from Dunkirk to Newcastle, in ballast. The yawl *Zephyr* was launched, but on boarding the brig the men were told by the master that all he wanted was a steam tug to tow his vessel into harbour. The beachmen duly fetched the tug *Emperor*. Robert George Jnr, for the Caister men, told the tale and said they would accept a third of what was awarded. Mr Preston, the advocate appearing for the vessel's owners, claimed that the service had been nothing more than a normal case of towage warranting a little extra for night work, and that attempts to make more of it were a disgrace to the town. The overall award was £25 with court costs. It was too small a sum to warrant an entry in the Company accounts.

That the Caister men decided to work with the tugs rather than oppose them, proved highly beneficial in April 1864 when the *Garland* of Hamburg, from Calcutta to Dundee, with jute and linseed oil, got stranded on the Cross Sand. She was assisted off by the Caister men in the yawls *Zephyr* and *Eclat*, and four Yarmouth steam tugs, which towed her to Lowestoft. The cargo was worth £7,000 and the vessel's insurers paid £1,310 in salvage. The beachmen must have received a good part of this for the amount entered into the accounts for the boat was £103.15s.1d.

Long before the arrival of specialist lifesaving equipment, the beachmen saved many seafarers using their own boats, none more so than the Caister men, in their yawl *Storm*. Early in 1830 the Norwegian Ship *Neptunus* was wrecked on Scroby, on a voyage from Salo to Rotterdam with brandy. The dispersed cargo was entered into the Admiralty Court by a number of salvors then auctioned. After the deduction of charges the salvors received 2/5ths of the appraised value of £1,144.15s.7d. but in addition the Court made a special award of £15 to Henry Key and his twelve man crew as a reward for their services in going off to the ship and 'saving the lives of the master and crew and bringing them safe on shore'.[39] Key received £3, the others £1 each.

Three years later, in March 1833, their stock rose even higher when the barque *Crawford*, from Hamburg, bound for London, with a cargo of 40 horses, ran onto the Haisborough Sand. After beating with great violence she was forced over into deep water, with the loss of her rudder. Seeing her hold filling fast the crew abandoned ship. Not long afterwards two of her three boats, with the captain's wife, niece and ten of the crew aboard, were passed by a Palling yawl, which they hailed only to find that the beachmen totally ignored them. Captain Sandford, in the third boat, returned to the barque and offered the Palling men 20 guineas to pick up the women. According to the newspaper reporter, 'The wretched thirst of gain or plunder overcame the splendid feeling of humanity; they were left to the mercy of the sea in a sinking boat. The Caister boatmen, with humanity highly praiseworthy, succeeded in reaching them and brought them safely on shore...'.[40] Ironically the ship soon became a wreck and the Palling men had to be rescued by that much-decorated lifesaver, Lieut. Thomas Leigh, in the Winterton lifeboat.

More praise was to follow. On the 21st February 1835 the Norwich Mercury gave credit to the Yarmouth Young Company for saving the crew of the brig *Edgar*, which had been lost on Scroby. In the following edition a correction was made, for the rescue had been the work of the Caister men, 'whose character stands high for good conduct in saving lives at the risk of their own, and in preference to their own advantage in saving property. In the case in question, the Caister men were the first by three or four hours who got to the stranded vessel; they found her abandoned by the crew, whom they neither saw nor heard any thing of but picked them up afterwards in their own boats... In picking up the crew and saving their clothes they lost some time, which otherwise would have been employed in getting more of the property themselves before the Yarmouth or Winterton boats had arrived...'. [41]

29. A lively depiction of the use of Captain Manby's lifesaving mortar from a monument he erected in his own front garden.

30. Former Caister Chief Coastguard, Walter Brattle, kept the Ship Inn when this photo was taken around 1910.
Left to right; ——, Charlie Lacock, ——, Bertie 'Geesha' George, John 'Honks' Brown, John Batley, ——,
Walter Brattle. The significance of the medallion around Honks' neck is unclear.

In this way the beachmen continued to save lives, but the limitations of their boats led to the introduction of two types of specialist lifesaving equipment, the mortar line and the lifeboat. The mortar line was developed by Capt. George Manby and was first used on the 12th February 1808, when the seven man crew of the brig *Elizabeth* was rescued after she had grounded in a gale, 150 yards from Yarmouth beach. Mortars were quickly placed along the coast normally under the control of the Preventative Officers (Coastguards) and in their capable hands, many lives were saved from vessels stranded close to the shore.

In 1827 Manby published his observations on the saving of mariners from stranded vessels and in the pamphlet he listed rescues made on the East Norfolk coast using his mortar lines.[42] The total lives saved was 324, including, at Caister, seven rescued from a Swedish ketch on the 23rd November 1825 and a further five from the sloop *Faith* on the 19th February 1826. In fact Manby's apparatus had been placed at Caister as early as 1819, under the care of Thomas Clowes, but it is unclear who manned it until the arrival of the Coastguards four years later. In 1851 the Caister Coastguards had at their disposal 12 Dennett 9lb rockets, supplied in 1846, and a 24lb mortar, claimed to have saved many lives, although it was noted that 'several of the rockets have burst'.[43] This echoes problems that were experienced on the 21st November 1840. During severe weather several vessels got into difficulties in the Roads, including the *St Rollux*, which had grounded close to the shore at Caister. The Coastguard fired two rockets, but neither left the ground. A line was eventually secured to the vessel and all but one of the crew saved.

While the coastguards actively tried to save life their primary purpose was the prevention of smuggling. The end of the French Wars saw a strengthening of both the land and seaborne branches of the Preventative Service, assisted by the fact that the Navy now had men and ships to spare. In 1822 the service was re-organised to improve efficiency, with the new force being called the Coastguard. This term encompassed the land-based preventative water-guard, the revenue cruisers and the mounted guard or riding officers, although the latter were greatly reduced once the coastguard stations became operational.

Coastguards were first stationed at Caister in 1823. Two years later their watch-house and boathouse were built on the dunes, to the north of the Cart Gap. The initial complement of this station was a chief officer, a chief boatman, a commissioned boatman and three ordinary boatmen. The first chief officer, Josh Warren was quickly replaced by William Osborne before two naval lieutenants, William Fowler and Henry Baillie, followed one another. In October 1828 John Brock took over the station and remained in post until his retirement in 1854, a remarkable 26 years. The reason this was remarkable was that coastguards, especially chief officers, were rarely allowed to stay at one station long, as this could lead to a level of familiarity, which might render them ineffective in their pursuit of smugglers. Fraternisation did, however, take place with coastguards, and their children, marrying into local families and others returning to Caister on retirement.

Brock was an authority figure, being a Sea Reeve between 1830 and 1834. In 1851 he is recorded as living near the church, well away from the sea. This may have been his way of avoiding potential clients or merely a question of finding a house and neighbours to reflect his status. Throughout this period the other coastguards were billeted in cottages around the village, mostly near the beach.

Two other coastguards left their mark on Caister, James Sneller and Richard Real. Dover born Sneller arrived from Winterton as a commissioned boatman in October 1835, remaining in the

31. Memorial to John Sneller who died in 1894. The Anchor and Cable motifs denote that the deceased was a seaman.

32. Memorial to former Chief Coastguard Richard Real, who died in 1896.

33. Possibly the earliest photograph (with **45)** of a Caister lifeboat, the *James Pearce Birmingham No.2,* c1870.
Coxswain Philip George is to be seen tenth from the right.

village until 1842, when he was posted to Skegness, on promotion to chief boatman. He brought with him a wife, who he had married in Winterton, and four children. On his retirement in 1854, as chief boatman in charge at Donna Nook, Lincolnshire, he chose to return to Caister. His two sons, John and Charles, both settled in the village, John becoming a master mariner in the merchant service and Charles, after a spell in the Navy, a prominent fisherman/beachman. Such was the esteem in which the latter was held that in 1887, when lifeboat coxswain, Philip George, lay dying he sent for Charles Sneller to replace him, but Sneller was too ill at the time. The position went to James Haylett Junior as his father, Jimmy, declined to take it on as he felt he was too old. Sneller did eventually become coxswain, albeit in a brief acting capacity after the 1901 disaster.

Richard Real was born in Newquay, Cornwall. After several years at Kessingland, he became chief boatman in charge of the Caister Station in 1851. He brought several daughters with him, one of whom, Mary Ann, married James Juby George in 1859 and another, Jane, married Walter Haylett, the well known fishing boat owner, in 1868.

Surprisingly, given the later prominence of the station, Caister was late in acquiring a lifeboat, with Winterton and Yarmouth stealing a march by some 20 years. Perhaps it was because the Caister men so successfully saved life in their yawl *Storm*. Whatever the reason for this omission it was rectified in the 1840s. In September 1841 the schooner *Surprise*, of Jersey, became a total wreck on the North Scroby, but the Caister men only managed to save one of her crew. As a result an appeal was launched for a lifeboat to be placed at Caister, but it did not bear fruit until 1845.

On January 4th that year the Norfolk Chronicle described how a large number of previously windbound vessels had set sail from the Roads and 'the German Ocean as far as the eye could reach, presented a beautiful appearance; as it is computed that from 1500 to 2000 vessels passed Yarmouth on that day'.

Later that month the news was quite different. On Sunday 26th January, a very heavy gale blew in from the north-west and at daybreak the beachmen at Yarmouth and Caister could see no fewer than five brigs in distress, four on Scroby and one on the Barber. Yawls were launched and crews saved, but unfortunately the Yarmouth Star Company yawl *Phoenix* was driven against the side of a brig and dashed to pieces with the loss of six of her crew.[44]

Shortly afterwards insinuations were made about the Caister men's failure to launch their new lifeboat. This prompted Thomas Clowes to leap to their defence and his letter to the Chronicle gives a colourful account of the arrival of the lifeboat. After extolling the virtues of the Caister beachmen as lifesavers, something he claimed to have observed for over 20 years, he described their six-hour struggle with the raging sea in the yawl *Storm*. They had attended three vessels and saved the nine-man crew of the *Elizabeth* of Scarborough. He then wrote of the lifeboat in the following terms; 'The Life Boat at Caister was brought here on the 6th January last, from Bacton. On the 7th I was informed she was landed on the beach, and requested to allow it with a shed to be built and placed on my land; this was the first intimation I had that a life boat was to come to Caister, not having heard one word of it before. You may easily conceive my surprise thereat. I immediately went and found two country carpenters with the boat and her materials, and also the materials for a shed, on the beach. The men informed me they were come to build the shed, and leave the boat; whereupon I fixed on a place that was considered by the beachmen most proper to erect the shed. The carpenters in a few days built the shed, and went home. The boat is a small one, about two-thirds the size of the Yarmouth boat, out of repair, and leaky. In landing her at Caister she was damaged, being laden with the materials and stores for the shed…The beachmen put her off to sea three days before the late gale to try her, and found her so leaky and unfit for the

34. The Rev. George Steward. Rector of Caister from 1829 until his death in 1878. He was secretary of the local lifeboat committee and supporter of the beachmen.

35. Dr. William Case, Secretary of the local lifeboat committee.

36. 'The Rush for the Lifeboat', from a drawing by C.J. Staniland, 1885.

intended service, they would not risk their lives in her'. [45]

Understandably the beachmen would not launch this ex Bacton boat, continuing to prefer their yawl *Storm* for lifesaving, a point reinforced by the fact that the Company accounts for 1845 show three entries for money paid for use of the *Storm* for saving men. Later that year the Rector of Caister, the Reverend George Steward, presented the Beach Company with 38 cork life preservers, 'in testimony of his sincere regard for theire temporal and spiritual welfare'.

The situation was rectified in March 1846 when a new lifeboat was stationed at Caister, under the auspices of the Norfolk Association for Saving the Lives of Shipwrecked Mariners. This 42 foot boat was designed by William Teasdell and built at Yarmouth by Branford. The sequence of events is recorded in the Company accounts in two laconic entries; 1844 'W Knowles Expenses at Bacton 5s.4d' and 1846 'Expenses at Yarm Life Boat 5s.2d'.

This boat was to see service at Caister until 1865, surviving the takeover in 1857 by the R.N.L.I. It was never given a name, the term lifeboat being sufficient for these early boats.   The first coxswain was probably Benjamin George Hodds.[46]

There is no definitive list of services, nor record of lives saved, while this lifeboat was the responsibility of the Norfolk Association, but the newspapers fill in some of the gaps. In December 1847 the crew of the *Darlington Packet* was saved from Scroby by the lifeboat and landed at

Winterton. More useful details are provided by the report of the rescue of the crew of the Portuguese Schooner *Propheta*. In December 1858 this vessel left Leith for Lisbon, with coal, but unfortunately grounded on Scroby. The lifeboat was launched, under coxswain Robert George Junior, and succeeded in saving the crew using a line from the boat. The newspaper reporter commented that, 'This is the fourteenth time in which George has gone out with the life-boat, and tenth in which he has been instrumental in saving life. The promptitude with which the life-boat was launched is highly creditable to those who manned it, four or five of whom, we understand, had only that day come into the harbour to make up their fishing.[47]

From 1849 the Company accounts show regular income for manning the lifeboat but, compared to the Company's boats, it does not appear to have been launched much, probably because the Norfolk Association required two shares of any salvage money awarded when the lifeboat was used. This did not change after the R.N.L.I. took over in December 1857, for between 1858 and 1865 the Company accounts show only nine salvage payments for work involving use of the lifeboat. Over the same period the yawl *Zephyr* received income from 80 services, *Eclat* 51, *Glance* 14, *Red Jacket* 3, the gig *Kitty* 7, *Hero* 12, *Dart* 2, and *Notus* 2. These figures demonstrate that as long as the beachmen had their own boats they were reluctant to use the lifeboat, something that would not change until the lifeboat was the only boat available to them.

Having said this some salvage cases, using the lifeboat, are worthy of note. In January 1858 the brig *Hilda*, from Odessa, for Hull, with barley, was struck by a heavy sea near Scroby. The Caister lifeboat was launched and, together with a Yarmouth steam tug, rendered assistance. The Company accounts show boat money of £4.7s.8d., although this has been crossed out. In March

37. Lifeboats and beach boats on Caister beach, 1893. The two men in conversation are, on the left, Frank Clowes and on the right Jimmy Haylett. The boats from left to right are either the yawl *Eclat* or *Glance,* and the lifeboats *Covent Garden* and *Beauchamp*.

38. Model of the yawl *Glance*, now in the lifeboat Visitor Centre. Between 1859 and 1890 she had a remarkable record of success at the Yarmouth Roads Regattas.

that same year there was an Adjudication hearing relating to the brig *Pytho*, which was spotted totally dismasted, close to breakers, to the north of Scroby. She was displaying a distress signal. The Caister men launched the lifeboat and boarded the vessel. Eventually a steam tug arrived and towed the brig into Yarmouth Harbour. The award was £106, together with £5.10s. for the loss of the lifeboat's anchor and warp.

In July 1862 there was a rare incident, which showed that the lifeboat was not always the safest place to be. At two o'clock on the 16th a storm struck Caister beach. Robert George, James Webster and two young boys named Wickerson and Golder were sheltering under the bows of the lifeboat when she was struck by lightning. All of them were rendered senseless for a short time. George, the veteran migrant from Winterton, sustained injuries to a leg and a foot, which were scorched in several places. The boat was not damaged, but her mast was 'burst from head to heel, and a long splinter driven out of it'.

The work of the beachmen was hard and dangerous, but the various marine regattas offered them the opportunity to pit their wits against their rivals in less desperate circumstances. Regattas were held at Yarmouth between 1830 and 1910 and the Caister men regularly took part. They were fairly low-key affairs until the coming of the railways in the mid-1840s, which brought large numbers of day-trippers, not so much to view the racing, but to have a good time on the beach, where other entertainments abounded. This attitude was not surprising for the events at sea were slow and very difficult to understand.

There were usually six to eight matches at each regatta, the first nearly always being a yacht race. Yawl races followed and were generally considered to be the most interesting of the day, as they were keenly contested. Both races were sailed around a double triangular course of some six to eight miles, making a total distance of 20 miles in all. The faster yawls could cover the distance in three hours, but some would take as long as five. The races were sailed on a handicap basis, an allowance of 30 seconds per foot being made.

The pattern of the yawl races closely mirrored the fortunes of the beach companies. Until 1843 the newspapers only reported the placed boats and these all came from the Yarmouth companies. The first Caister yawl to be mentioned was the *Fox*, unplaced in the 1844 Regatta. She competed as Caister's entry until 1852, achieving a creditable three second places and a third. But with the Caister men lifesaving always came first as an incident at the 1847 Regatta demonstrates. According to the Norwich Mercury, 'Just after the Fox yawl was leaving her moorings, a man, whose boat had been engaged by a pleasure party, most foolishly ran his boat under the Fox's bows, and was cut in pieces and sunk in about 15 feet (of) water, precipitating the passengers, who were mostly females, into the water. The crew of the Fox in the most praiseworthy manner rendered assistance to rescue the crew of the boat, and all were taken safe to land. By this means the Fox, which had been, well placed, and was a leading boat, unfortunately lost the race'.[48]

Over the years the yawls *Eclat*, *Red Jacket* and *Zephyr* put in the occasional appearance, but it was the *Glance* that placed Caister on the map, as far as yawl races were concerned. She first appeared in the 1858 Regatta, finishing last, but between 1859 and 1890 she achieved a remarkable eight firsts, four seconds and two thirds, with firsts being worth £15, seconds £10, and thirds £5. The reporter of the 1874 event lamented that the *Glance* was the only boat to compare with those from the past.

In 1875, despite the *Glance* driving onto the beach and thus being unplaced, a reporter

39. Caister lifeboats, c1875. The *Godsend ex Boys* is on the left, the *Covent Garden ex James Pearce* on the right.

40. Caister beach village, 1976. These detached houses back onto Clay Road and front what was the Common.

commented that, 'The deeds of the Caister beachmen in saving life and property are known throughout the country, and although the men yesterday were engaged in what to them was mere holiday pastime, their *physique* showed immediately that they were men accustomed to rough work, involving frequent peril to life and limb. Among the crew who manned the Caister yawl, the Glance, were to be found men whose career in the service of humanity has afforded remarkable instances of daring and self possession in times of imminent peril. Such men as Haylett and George of the Caistor Company of beachmen are, however, but types of their class, and their compeers, both in skill and daring, are happily to be found not only among beachmen on this exposed portion of the Norfolk coast, but in many other localities'.[49]

The following year, 'After the conclusion of the yawl match, J.D. Clowes Esq., Lord of the Manor of Caister, entertained the Caister boatmen by giving them a bountiful repast at one of his residences in Norfolk Square', (Yarmouth).[50] The *Glance* was Caister's most successful yawl until sold to new owners in Southend, in 1902. She ended her days as the pleasure boat *Royal Sovereign* at Skegness.

Races were also arranged for beach company gigs, coastguard boats, and Trinity Service boats. On six occasions lifeboats were put through their paces, with the Caister boat taking part in 1851 and 1854. In 1851 she came first out of nine in two categories, hoisting of sails and sailing, and second in the other two, rowing and sailing while full of water. This placed her first overall. In 1854 she lost out to the newly arrived California lifeboat *Prince Albert*, but was first in the sailing while full of water trial.

Between 1811 and 1861 the parish population of Caister more than doubled, rising from 629 to 1203. Similarly the number of houses rose from 135 to 311, but the overall shape of the village remained much the same, as most of the growth took place in the newly created 'beach village'.

By 1861 around 320 people were living in what is now Victoria Street, Clay Road, and the adjacent parts of Beach Road and Tan Lane, an area that is now considered to be the old village.

Mention has already been made of the fact that Victoria Street existed in the 18th century, but by 1813 only the west side had been developed. At that time the people living there had an uninterrupted view across the Common towards the sea. The Common was part of the manorial holding of the Clowes family and they were responsible for creating the remainder of the beach village.

In 1839 a map of Caister was drawn for tithe purposes. It shows that by then the eastern side of Victoria Street was built up. The accompanying documentation gives the owners and occupiers of this street and whereas the west side was characterised by the old Caister surnames of Brady, Davey, Purdy, Horth and Green, the east side was home to Winterton migrants Ben Hodds, William Olley, Robert George, John George, Thomas George and John Haylett. By 1851 this was called East Street, in 1861 it is referred to as Back Street and in 1871 Horn Street. It later became Victoria Street.

In 1851 some 33 families were living in East Street and a further 13 were described as 'near the Common', or what was to become Clay Road. This road was laid out in the 1840s and by 1861, when it was called 'Newtown', there were 34 families living there. By 1871 it had become Clay Road, presumably taking its name from the contrasting nature of the imported road surface. The houses on the eastern side have their backs to the road in order to face what was the Common. Seafaring migrants, mostly from Winterton, dominated the beach village.

Also in the early 1850s a row of cottages were built to the north of Beach Road, facing the sea. This is where Jimmy Haylett and his brother Isaiah lived when first they came to Caister.

41. A group of people outside the Ship beerhouse, c1895.

Back row, left to right; Paul George, James Haylett Junior, ——, William 'Hilton' Brown, ——, ——, Charles 'Shah' Brown. Front row; Robert 'Puddens' Brown, 'Tight' Hayward, Susanna Bonney George (the licensee), Sergeant-major Travers.

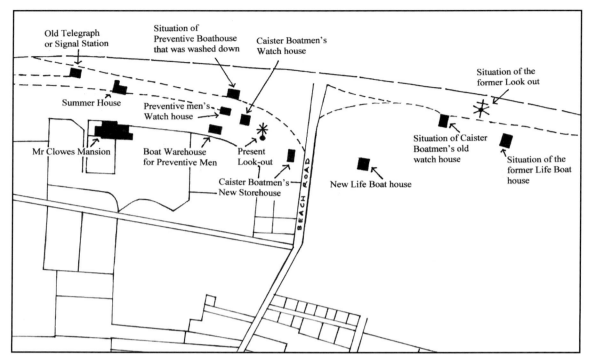

42. Sketch map of Caister beach in 1851. It shows the disposition of Beach Company and coastguard structures, and the Manor buildings. Taken from NRO Y/PH 1035.

The beach village lay between Beach Road and Tan Lane, the latter named after the leather tannery that stood in the High Street, more or less where the public toilets are today. In 1851 the tanyard house was occupied by saddler George Edwards.[51]

Until 1830 the Caister seafarers frequented the Lord Nelson Tavern, in Beach Road, but that year the Beer Act gained the Royal assent, creating a new type of drinking establishment, the beer house. These were intended to wean people off gin. They were not to open on Sundays and their keepers were only permitted to sell beer and cider. In 1836 White's Norfolk Directory lists two beer house keepers in Caister, Mary Blythe and Robert George. The one run by Robert George was set up in the house he had built in 1815. By 1868 at least it was called The Ship. The George family kept The Ship until the end of the 19th century, it passing in 1867 to Robert's son Aaron and then in 1888 to Aaron's widow, Susannah Bonney. After her death it was granted a full licence and became an inn. Aaron and Susannah's son, Joseph Bonney George, was also in the licensed trade, keeping the Lord Nelson from the 1880s until just before the First World War.

During the early part of this period there was little in the way of development between the village and the beach save Davey's farm and the East Windmill. The mill was built around 1818 and was owned and run by the Davey family. Until Beach Road was built up the mill stood in splendid isolation, taking full advantage of the coastal winds.

Beyond the mill, on the high sand dune ridge protecting the village, stood a number of buildings and structures associated with the beachmen and the coastguards. In 1851 Thomas Clowes took a former highway surveyor, named Beck, to court for taking stones off the beach without permission. As part of the legal process, a plan was drawn showing the disposition of the various buildings, both past and present. The witnesses generally agreed that the beach to the north of the Gap had been considerably eroded, but that that to the south had expanded. This centuries old process of erosion and deposition was to continue into the middle of the 20th century.

As far as the Beach Company is concerned the plan shows a movement of buildings from the south to north of the Gap, perhaps for reasons of convenience, as erosion seems not to have been an issue. The Company accounts throw some light on this process, but clarity is hindered by the fact that the buildings do not bear consistent names in the entries. In 1846 a mast was brought from Yarmouth for a new lookout and £21.3s.4d. was spent on a 'new shed'. This was probably a new watch-house as the storehouse was being described as new in 1851. In 1849 a new lifeboat shed was built closer to the Gap and the original one was demolished.

The Company accounts contain many enigmatic references to building work. In January 1857, 7,000 bricks were bought, but their purpose is not specified. A new shed was built in 1860. Perhaps this was the one, mentioned in the 1861 census, situated close to the parish boundary with Yarmouth. By 1863 entries were being made in relation to coal for the North Court, and also for a South Court, but references to the latter one cease in 1864. It seems likely that, for a brief period, the Company divided its resources in order to be more competitive with its neighbours. There are numerous entries concerning repairs to the lookout and a new one was built in 1864.

The Coastguard buildings are shown as a watch-house and a boat warehouse, but the earlier brick built boathouse of 1825 had been washed away.

Throughout this period Caister's 60 or so deep-sea fishermen continued to be employed in the Spring mackerel and the Autumn herring fisheries. Many of them skippered the Yarmouth boats, a fact confirmed by Nall, who commented; 'Almost all the beachmen in these villages (Winterton, Caister, California and Newport) are either masters or mates of herring boats'.[52]

Deep sea fishing boat owning was a different matter. In August 1845, Caister miller, John

43. Yarmouth Herring lugger unloading at the Quay, 1829. Engraving by E.W. Cooke.

44. 'Longshore boats on Caister Beach, c1910. In the background, from left to right is the Beach Company watch-house, the Coastguard lookout and the Manor House hotel.

Wincott, bought the 30-year-old lugger *Victory*, but sold her the following May. In 1845 he also became part owner, with three Yarmouth men of the newer lugger, *Coriander*, but he seems to have been no more than the man providing the capital.

Caister farmer, Clement Burton, bought the fishing lugger *Ranger* in 1841 and ran her for a number of years, with John Burton and Dennis George as her skippers. He sold her in 1855 to Yarmouth, wine and spirit merchant, John Makepiece.

In 1844, John Curtis, a Cantley fisherman, bought the *Seven Brothers* with mortgage money. When in 1848 he defaulted on the payments, ownership passed to Thomas Clowes, who kept her until 1852, but it is unclear how the boat was managed at this time.

By and large these boats represent investments by Caister landsmen, the fishermen of the village not yet entering into the risky business of deep-sea fishing boat ownership, all, that is, except one. In May 1862, Jacob George, together with John Brett, bought the *Spray* from Yarmouth man John Playford. By then Brett was living in Yarmouth and in 1866 he sold his half share to George, who was still described as a fisherman of Caister. She seems to have been run from Yarmouth and by the end of the 1860s George too had migrated there. The *Spray* remained in the family until sold in 1895 by Jacob's widow Ann Eliza, having been converted to dandy rig in 1884.

'Longshore fishing continued to be practised from the beach and crew lists for 1845 reveal eight boats and their master/owners, namely the *Dart* (John Haylett), *Elixa* (Benjamin Hodds), *Gem* (Robert George), *George and Jessy* (Thomas Horth), *Lowland Lass* (James Vincent), *Mary Ann* (William Munford), *Young Thomas* (Thomas George), and *William and Mary* (William Hodds).[53]

4. 1865-1914

On the 25th October 1865 a 42 foot lifeboat was launched from the Yarmouth yard of Mills & Blake to replace the 1846 Caister boat, which had become unseaworthy. As the Birmingham lifeboat fund had provided the money, the new boat was called the *James Pearce, Birmingham No 2*.

Her first service took place that very same day, for as she set sail for her new station the crew spotted the schooner *Maria*, of Hull, in trouble on Scroby and quickly went to her assistance. Salvage was paid and the Company accounts show boat money of £2.18s.1d.

Two years later a second station became operational with the arrival of the 32-foot surf lifeboat *Boys*, named as such because she had been purchased with donations collected by Routledges's Magazine for Boys. She was deemed necessary as the larger boat was designed for offshore work and could not easily be deployed close to the shore.

Her first service was to the Norwegian schooner *Assistant*, of Stavanger, which became stranded on the Barber on the 25th November 1867. The *Boys* stood by while beachmen in the yawls *Zephyr* and *Eclat* carried out the salvage work, the accounts showing boat money of £13.15s. and a further 16s. for the anchor.

Over the next decade these lifeboats were launched on average five to six times a year, rescuing over 300 souls whilst, at the same time, earning useful salvage money for saving many of the vessels involved, but they were still not the beachmens' first choice of boat. Over the same period the yawls *Zephyr, Eclat, Glance* and *Red Jacket* were used three times as much, although the latter was rarely launched as she was considered to be 'a bit cranky'.[54]

The late 1860s/early 1870s were the best years for the Company, a fact borne out by the cost of shares, which can be taken as a reasonable indicator of expected returns. In the 1830s shares

45. The Caister lifeboat *James Pearce, Birmingham No 2*, c1870. The photograph was taken at the same time as **33**.

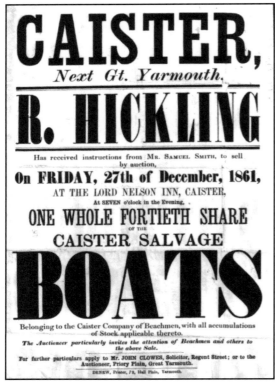

46. Auction Poster for the sale of a share in the Caister Beach Company, 1861. The share belonged to Samuel Smith and was sold to James Haylett Junior for £84.

47. Caister Beachman and Yarmouth fish salesman Dennis George 1821-1907.

changed hands for £10-£12. The 1840s and 1850s produced an average of £45, whereas during the 1860s shares sold for £85 with, in 1869, James George Green King paying John Plummer £100 for his share, a transaction which would prove to be the death of him. In 1877 Beauchamp victim William Wilson bought the share of Sarah George's late husband for £75, but after that prices fell to £20-£30.

On the 19th December 1868 the Norwich Mercury was pleased to report that, 'THE BEACHMEN at this station (Caister) have been very fortunate of late with salvage cases, and several large sums have been paid to them. It was not long since we reported that they had received the magnificent sum of £2,055, to divide between themselves and three tugs, for assisting the s.s. Ganges off the Hasborough sands, and now this week they have been paid £550, for services rendered to the barque Hurfruen, of Sandijford, timber laden, from Lulea to Antwerp, which had got upon the Cross Sands a fortnight back. It will be remembered that on that occasion another timber laden ship was capsized on the same sand and, but for the presence of the Caister life boat, nine lives would have been lost, for saving which the royal National Life Boat Institution pay £25'.

Having written this the reporter took pains to place these windfalls in context by adding, 'All this must not, however, be taken as a fair average of what beachmen can earn in winter. In some years they don't receive 4s. a week per man, and as yet they have had no opposition this season from their Californian neighbours, whose life boat had been under repairs'.

Besides these spectacular payments earned by the large lifeboat, the *Zephyr* secured £100 for services to the brig *Rover*, £15 for the schooner *Hertha* and an unspecified sum for the schooner *Calmack*. The *Eclat* received £165 for the barque *Voltigeur*, together with unspecified amounts for the brig *Ferris* and the schooner *Lord Coke*, while the *Glance* earned £192 for the barque *Conolour*. The large lifeboat also secured £153.10s. for the schooner *Wave* and £90 for the barque *Balder*.

This was a very good year for the Caister Company, but the beachmen had a grievance. They were annoyed with the way the local correspondent of the Norwich Mercury was reporting their activities and as a result they and their children had been hooting at him and his family, 'on their way to and from church on Sundays, week-day evening meetings, and at other times'.[55] Defending his paper a reporter wrote in justification, 'We have always been pleased to notice the daring and bravery of the beachmen in real danger, and while we have been careful to avoid publishing what is untrue, we have at the same time not shrunk from reporting the facts of the case, whatever they may be, and so long as we can confidently rely on the veracity of a statement about any matter of public interest, we shall continue to publish it as we have hitherto done, notwithstanding the disgraceful proceedings of many Caister beachmen to endeavour to deter our correspondent from communicating to us what is occurring at Caister'.[56] The reception this received in the Company watch-house can easily be imagined.

The year 1869 was another good one for the Company. On the 15th February the barque *Eliza Caroline*, of London, sailed from Shields for Carthagena, with a cargo of coke, shot and Armstrong guns. While working through the Roads she became stranded on the inner spit of Scroby. After failing to work her off the master burned a flare and the Caister men, in the yawl *Eclat* and the

48. Caister lifeboatmen alongside the surf lifeboat *Beauchamp, 1892.*

Back row, left to right; Frank Clowes (Hon. Secretary), Solly Brown, Charlie Sneller, Ben Read, Jimmy Haylett. Middle row; Billy Wilson, James Haylett junior, Walter Haylett. Front row, George Smith Haylett, Harry Knights, Joe Julier, Ben Kettle.

49. The s.s.*Lady Flora* stranded on Caister Beach after running aground on 29th April 1869. Successfully refloated on 8th July 1869, with 3,000 people looking on, she was lost at sea later the same year.

large lifeboat, were soon alongside to render assistance. They were quickly followed by the California lifeboat and both groups of beachmen were engaged. As it was night-time little could be done other than take the barque's crew ashore, but at daybreak four tugs came out from Yarmouth and the *Eliza Caroline* was beached near the Britannia Pier. For their efforts the Caister and California beachmen shared a very handy £1,600.

A week later the large lifeboat was launched to the full rigged ship *Hannah Petersen*, of Bergen, bound for Odessa, with upwards of 1,500 tons of coal, which had been loaded at Shields. She had entered the Roads on the 4th February and on taking up a berth had collided with the brig *Mabel*. On the Friday after the collision a gale sprang up and there was some concern as to what would happen to the 'big ship'. On the Monday she was still at her mooring, but labouring heavily. Later that day she was driven onto the beach, abreast the workhouse. The lifeboat landed the 20-man crew, and they were taken to the Sailor's Home.

On April 29th the steamship *Lady Flora*, of Hull, became stranded on Caister beach. Hydraulic cranes and 120 men were employed, at a cost of £2,000, to raise her four feet above the beach. She was successfully refloated on the 8th July, with 3,000 people looking on, but later that same year she was lost at sea. The surf lifeboat, had stood by but the Beach Company does not seem to have been directly involved in the salvage of what was a big prize on its very doorstep.

November saw the Caister men in the Adjudication Court concerning a claim for services to the brigantine *Letitia*. She had first been salvaged by the brig *Caroline*, but when in turn that vessel had got into difficulties off Scroby, the Caister men had been employed by the master of the *Letitia*, on an agreement for £180. They had summoned a steam tug, which towed her into harbour. The crew of the *Caroline* was awarded £60 and the tug, together with the Caister men, £70.

By 1875 the lifesaving reputation of the Caister men was well established, but the events of that year served to raise it still higher while bringing into focus the two leading men at the time, Philip George and Jimmy Haylett.

On the 29th January, during thick weather, the Italian barque *Conessa Padre*, bound for Aberdeen, with a cargo of bone ash, became stranded on the Cross Sand. Distress rockets were fired from the St. Nicholas lightship and, 'The Caister men, ever on the alert for the slightest sign, no sooner saw the signals than they mustered their lifeboat crew, and in a very short time were on their way to the vessel....'.[57] Having made an agreement with the master for £625, they brought out more men and, after labouring all day, got her off. Steam tugs took her to Harwich.

No sooner had they completed the task when fresh distress signals were seen coming from the Newarp lightship. 'The Caister men undeterred by the labour they had undergone, and with their brace of irrepressibles, Haylett and George, as usual to the fore, started off in the lifeboat for the new venture'. Heading for the scene the crew soon discovered that there had been a collision between a steamer and a large full rigged ship, the latter sustaining a great deal of damage. She was the *Oriental*, from Shields, bound for Carthagena, with a cargo of coal. Her master immediately accepted the Caister men's offer of assistance and, after fending off a crew from California, they navigated her safely into the Roads, from where she too was towed to Harwich by steam tugs. The boat money of £15.6s.2½d. suggests the salvage payment received was even higher than that for the Italian barque.

Several lucrative services followed and many more lives were saved in gallant rescues, prompting photographers Sawyer & Bird to take a photograph of Caister's finest and exhibit it on the South Pier, in August, during the Yarmouth Regatta. It was reported in the Yarmouth Independent that, 'The services rendered by the Caister boatmen during the career of their leaders, Haylett and George,

CAISTER BOATMEN.—A fine cabinet picture has been issued from the studio of Messrs. Sawyers of King-street, giving very faithful portraits of Haylett and George, the two prominent members of the Caister lifeboat company of beachmen. The picture in question was exhibited on the South-pier, during the recent Regatta sports, where it attracted much attention. Apart from the merits of the picture as exhibiting a high stage of photographic art, interest was attached to it from the announcement appended beneath that Haylett and George had been instrumental in saving 51 lives since November last. The frequency of wrecks off this coast, and the gallant exertions of the Caister beachmen in saving life and property are matters of more than mere local history. Residents are so familiar with life-saving incidents arising in their immediate vicinity, that they are accepted as a matter of course. The services rendered by the Caister boatmen during the career of their leaders, Haylett and George, have been, however, of great importance, and we question whether two men can be found on the English coast who have passed through more scenes of peril in the pursuit of their calling than the two men whose likenesses have been so admirably pourtrayed by Messrs. Sawyer. We are accustomed to read of many acts of heroism performed by the Deal boatmen in saving life and property from the dangerous Goodwin sands. In the majority of their cases, meritorious as they may be, the men are towed out to sea by powerful steamers placed at their disposal, but off this coast our lifeboat crews have no such assistance available. In the majority of cases they have to depend on themselves, and in many a stormy night have to feel their way with great peril over the outlying sands on the coast before their assistance can be rendered available.

50. A fine photograph of Philip George and Jimmy Haylett taken in 1875. The context is explained in the article from the Yarmouth Independent of 14th August 1875.

have been, however, of great importance, and we question whether two men can be found on the English coast who have passed through more scenes of peril in the pursuit of their calling than the two men whose likenesses have been so admirably pourtrayed by Messrs Sawyer'.[58]

On the 21st October the large lifeboat was launched to the barque *Young England* after a crewman had swam ashore to get help. He was the sole survivor of the ship's boat, which had contained 12 of the crew, but four remained on the vessel. In difficult circumstances the Caister men managed to pluck them from a certain death. In response to this dramatic rescue, John Clowes, wrote a long letter to the press in praise of the Caister men, pointing out, 'that to accomplish thus much, on this bleak and excessively dangerous coast, they continually are called upon during dark nights, when nothing beyond the white foam of the surf creates some feeble revelation of any object at sea, the gale blowing furiously, with huge waves breaking all around, whilst at home, with bated breath as each gust of the tempest howls around the cottage, are wife and children, awaiting husbands and father's safe return'.[59]

Coincidently, alongside this letter was a report on the Caister men's rescue of seven from the brigantine *Harmston* in which the reporter commented that, 'The only reward these brave fellows will get in the ordinary way for their gallant conduct will be £25 from the Lifeboat Society for launching to the ship, but this will be a very inadequate remuneration for their praiseworthy services in saving the lives of seven men who would inevitably have been drowned had not the Caister men reached the vessel as they did'.[60]

This provoked further correspondence, not all of it favourable to the beachmen, with one of the anonymous writers, using the pseudonym VIGILANT, reporting that, 'I was waited upon by Haylett and George, and in describing the service they had just rendered Haylett complained of the small remuneration offered for life salvage, and stated that he and those associated with him were almost dispirited and beaten. To this George, who is I believe coxswain of the Caister lifeboat, made no reply, and his silence would therefore be taken as assent'.[61]

Clowes had also written again and in his later letter he referred to Philip George as the coxswain, and Jimmy Haylett, as 'the head man of the company, whose daring acts (notwithstanding his being afflicted with a large white tumour on his back, originating with the hardship he has endured), are well attested by the 540 lives they have saved...'.[62]

As the arguments raged over payment for 'life salvage' Philip George, the quiet one of the two, answered his critics in the only way he knew how, action. On the 19th November the schooner *Wild Wave* of Sunderland, with a cargo of bottles, was driven onto Caister beach, after having been in collision with the Cockle Lightship, during a gale. She was spotted by the coastguards and beachmen. With no hope of launching a lifeboat, the coastguards fired a number of rockets, but the schooner's crew could not secure the attached lines. The master was washed overboard and drowned and a lad was hit by the windlass and killed, but the other three crewmen managed to take to the mast. Led by Philip George and Chief Coastguard Samuel Bishop, a mixed group of beachmen and coastguards set about rescuing the three men by forming a human chain to pluck them from the water when the mast inevitably fell. For their heroic efforts Philip George and Samuel Bishop were both awarded the R.N.L.I.'s silver medal, Philip's being the first gallantry medal to be awarded to a Caister beachman. He was later to receive a second silver medal.

On the face of it the relationship between these two giants of the Caister Beach Company was one of mutual respect, but all was not quite what it seemed. Both men were migrants from Winterton who will have known each other since childhood, although Jimmy was the older by seven years. As made plain by John Clowes Jimmy was the headman of the company and was also 'the

51. Jimmy Haylett, c1905. The best-known Caister beachman.

52. Philip George, c1875. Caister lifeboat coxswain and Silver medal winner.

speaker', that is the man who told the tale in court to maximise the salvage awards. He was clearly a leader of men and a fine seaman. Philip, on the other hand, was the man elected to be the lifeboat coxswain, a position he held for over 20 years until shortly before his death, after illness, in 1888. Unless Jimmy did not wish to be the coxswain the implication is that Philip was an even better seaman. Jimmy outlived his colleague by nearly 20 years and in that time his exploits and his ability to tell the tale made him something of a legend, feted by all, but Philip's opinion of him was less enthusiastic. Appearing at the inquest into the death of the Caister men in the yawl *Zephyr II*, he was asked about the choice of coxswain, given that Jimmy had been at the tiller. His reply is instructive; 'We don't make any selection of coxswain on such occasions. As they scramble into the boat, the man who happens to be at the stern of the boat takes the helm… Mr. Haylett was not chosen because of his superior knowledge beyond the others of the company. All in this room have been coxswains in their time'.[63] This perhaps explains the tradition, in the George family, that Philip was Caister's finest beachman and that Jimmy's reputation in this respect was largely due to his longevity and way with words.

By the early 1880s the beach companies were struggling. They had flourished when large numbers of wooden sailing ships got into difficulties on, or around, the offshore sandbanks, with the beachmen having a virtual monopoly over the resultant savage work, or at least the ability to compete on equal terms with their rivals. As the 19th century progressed, so these advantages all but disappeared. Navigational aids, in the form of buoys and lightships, were introduced to pinpoint the sandbanks, steam power and iron ships replaced wooden sailing vessels, Navigation Acts improved safety at sea and the steam tug became a real competitor.

The town companies suffered greatly as a result, but the village companies fared better. Their beachmen could afford to treat salvage work as a supplement to their earnings in the deep-sea fisheries, an industry in which many of them were working as skippers or boat owners. In addition these companies learned to work with the steam tugs as they depended on each other. Large steamers, stranded on the sandbanks, needed beachmen to fetch tugs, affix hausers and shift cargo, and the beachmen in their turn would not have been able to handle these jobs without the pulling power of the tugs.

The problem was that although payments from salvage work involving steamers tended to be considerably higher than those for sailing ships, the number of casualties was far fewer. The Caister Beach Company accounts show that between 1842 and 1880 the annual entries for salvage services averaged 16, between 1880 and 1900, this had dropped to five and between 1900 and the outbreak of the First World War, they were lucky to get two.

This fall in income meant that many companies could no longer afford to maintain or replace their boats. Those that had them became more and more dependent on the use of the R.N.L.I. lifeboats. This was the case at Caister. In 1883 the large lifeboat, *James Pearce, Birmingham No 2*, which had been renamed *Covent Garden* in 1878, was replaced by a new boat, also called *Covent Garden*, in acknowledgement of the amount of money raised annually by that establishment.

She joined a fleet of boats comprising the yawls *Zephyr II, Eclat* and *Glance*, a gig, and the surf lifeboat *Godsend*, which until 1875 had been called the *Boys*. Two years later the Company experienced a tragedy, which reduced the fleet still further and took the lives of eight of the beachmen.

On the night of the 22nd July 1885 a schooner was spotted close to the Barber by the two-man watch, Philip George and James Haylett Junior. As they tracked her progress so she swung round,

53. The second *Covent Garden* lifeboat on launch day, 3rd November 1883.

54. 'On the Sands', from a drawing by C.J. Staniland, 1885. A mast stump, as depicted, was the cause of the *Zephyr II* disaster that year.

convincing Philip George that she had struck the outer edge of the sandbank. Haylett immediately rang the bell and hurried off to 'knock up' a crew and as the sea was calm and moonlit the yawl *Zephyr II* was the boat launched. The fifteen-man crew were in good spirits, laughing and joking amongst themselves. Jimmy Haylett was at the helm and as they approached the Barber he called out, 'Keep a lookout for the old stump', referring to the mast of a paving stone laden schooner, the crew of which had been saved by these very men nine years earlier. The words were scarcely out of his mouth when the yawl's port bow struck the mast and the boat was ripped open. Within two minutes the crew was struggling in the water.

Fortunately there was just enough time for the gear to be thrown overboard and this proved to be the survivors salvation. When Jimmy Haylett surfaced he grabbed hold of two oars to support himself, managing to lash them together with a scarf. Being close to the foremast he and his son Aaron, together with Joseph Haylett and William Knowles took hold of it and stayed afloat for a while, but the mast kept rolling over and while Aaron switched to his father's oars the other two drowned.

As the yawl went down, John George, the real hero of the calamity, stripped before swimming away, calling out as he did so, ' Fare you well my lads, I'm going to swim for the beach'. After a while he came across the Yarmouth shrimper, *The Brothers*, crewed by the Liffen brothers, Charles and Emmanuel. Clambering aboard George directed the shrimper to the scene of the disaster and one by one they picked up Robert Plummer, Aaron Haylett, Isaiah Haylett, George Haylett, Harry Russell and Jimmy Haylett. Eight other men were not so fortunate. At the subsequent inquest special praise was given to John George and the Liffen brothers for their prompt action.

The irony of this tragedy was not lost on Charles Staniland, who in a piece on the Norfolk and Suffolk type lifeboat for the English Illustrated Magazine observed, 'Almost as this paragraph was written comes the news that these gallant fellows – who have faced the heaviest gales on the east coast in their lifeboats, the *Birmingham, Covent Garden* and *Godsend*, and saved six or seven hundred lives (the highest record of any crew round the coast) and never lost a man – had gone out in their light yawl *Zephyr* to the relief of a schooner which had gone on the Barber Sand, and on a fine night in sight of shore (only about a mile) had lost eight men out of a crew of fifteen, leaving six widows and twenty-nine children'.[64] Caister mourned, but the Beach Company ranks were quickly filled and these hardy men continued their dangerous work.

The 1890s was the decade in which the lifeboats took over from the yawls as the boats of first choice. There were nine entries of boat money for the yawl *Eclat* and two for the *Glance*, but the lifeboats clocked up 19 between them, not to mention the launches where 'life salvage' was the outcome. The beachmen had in fact become the lifeboatmen.

During this decade both lifeboats were replaced. The surf boat *Boys/Godsend* had been at the No 2 station since its inception in 1867 and, although she had been improved in 1875, by the early 1890s she was well past her best. Accordingly a replacement was built, the ill-fated *Beauchamp*. Constructed by Critten at Yarmouth she was named after Sir Reginald Proctor Beauchamp, the major contributor to her cost, who formally inaugurated her at the station, on the 21st January 1892. In her time at Caister she was launched 81 times, saving 146 lives.

The high spot in her career was undoubtedly the service to the full rigged ship *Soudan*, at the

55. The surf lifeboat *Beauchamp* on launch day, 21st January 1892. The postcard was issued after the 1901 disaster, overprinted with 'Caister Life-boat disaster Nov. 14th 1901. The ill fated Beauchamp & Crew'.

56. The *Beauchamp* disaster, 1901. 'The crowd pulling the boat ashore'.

time considered to be the most difficult in living memory. On the 7th November 1896 this vessel became stranded on the outer edge of Scroby. The following morning, as the weather worsened, the Gorleston lifeboat, *Mark Lane*, took off 19 of her crew, leaving eight still on board. Luckily for them the *Beauchamp* had also launched to assist, but had had to fight her way over the Barber and across the broken water covering Scroby, with the lifeboatmen lashed to the boat to stop themselves being washed overboard. Using her sails and the services of a steam tug to get close, lines were thrown to bring the *Beauchamp* alongside, enabling the eight men to jump aboard. With the rescue accomplished the lifeboat made for Yarmouth harbour, where it was greeted by cheering spectators thronging the piers.

Unfortunately the *Beauchamp* will always be remembered for the tragedy that occurred on the night of the 13th November 1901, when nine Caister men lost their lives. The sequence of events, which led to the disaster started earlier that day when the Lowestoft smack *Buttercup*, with James Smith at the tiller, left the fishing grounds to return home. As the day wore on so the weather worsened until there was a galeforce wind accompanied by sleet. As the smack headed for the Cockle Light she shipped a heavy sea and bumped upon what proved to be the Barber. Fearing the worst Smith lit a flare, but after a while he managed to anchor the smack and ride out the storm until morning when he proceeded to Lowestoft, oblivious to the calamity his actions had provoked.

At Caister it was very dark and heavy breakers were beating onto the beach. Searching the inky blackness the men on watch spotted the flare and the two rockets sent up from the Cockle Lightship. Judging the casualty to be on the Barber the Company was quickly summoned and at about 11 o'clock they set about launching the *Beauchamp*. The sea kept beating them back, but the weary men persevered and, after three hours of strenuous effort and a change of crew, she was launched over the crashing surf.

Job done the wet and weary launchers trudged home or to the Company watch-house, while the *Beauchamp*, with Aaron Haylett at the helm, fought her way towards the Barber, the crew little knowing that their services were no longer necessary. After much effort, the lifeboat reached the

Barber = Sands

Sand, but it kept being swept back. Coxswain Haylett soon realised that he had problems, for when he tacked for the second time the *Beauchamp* failed to respond to the helm. Being close to the shore, he called out 'down mizzen' and put the helm up to make for the beach, but the lifeboat struck the ground and a huge wave caught her on the quarter and over she went, trapping her crew beneath her upturned hull.

It was three in the morning when on the beach Fred Haylett, one of Jimmy's grandsons thought he could hear voices coming from the darkness. He rushed to tell the other beachmen who, led by his grandfather, hurried down to the sea. Seeing someone struggling in the breakers, the old man grabbed hold of him only to find to his dismay, that it was his son-in-law Charlie Knights. The awful truth dawned as another of his grandsons, Walter Sequah Haylett, together with Jack Hubbard, were dragged ashore, but none of the other members of the 12 man crew managed to get out from under the boat alive. The nine men lost that morning, were two of Jimmy's sons, James and Aaron Haylett, his grandson Harry Knights, who was making his first trip, brothers William Hilton and Charles Shah Brown, Charles Bonney George, John Smith, George King and William Wilson.

Their loss had a devastating effect on the village, not only in terms of the people and the Beach Company, but also on the principal breadwinning activity of the Caister seafarers herring fishing. The Yarmouth Mercury reporter noted that, 'Most of the deceased were associated with drifters engaged in the herring fishery, and the glow around their glorious deaths is deepened by the fact that, though they were at home because the weather was too bad to prosecute their livelihood, they showed no hesitation in facing the elements the moment that life was in danger, and answered the

57. John Smith, 1858-1901. Lost in the *Beauchamp.*

58. William 'Billy' Wilson 1845-1901. Lost in the *Beauchamp.*

59. Jimmy Haylett wearing the R.N.L.I.'s gold medal presented to him by King Edward VII in 1902.

60. The poignant memorial to the men who lost their lives in the 1901 disaster. The position of the stones reflect where each man sat in the lifeboat.

summoning bell with the alacrity of the brave men they were'.[65]

Hilton Brown owned the drifter *Alpha* and his brother Shah was her skipper. Charles Bonney George skippered the drifter *Queen Alexandra* for Frank Clowes, and John Smith the *Snowdrop*. In fact the reason the *Beauchamp* had been chosen that night was because of the fishing for as Jimmy Haylett put it, 'during the three months of the fishing season, they made most use of the *Beauchamp* as she was a handier and lighter craft to handle, and they had a number of their men away on the fishing'. [66]

Jimmy Haylett, the old veteran, was the principal witness at the inquest and it was there that he replied when asked if it was likely that the lifeboatmen had given the smack up, 'No, they never give up. They would have been there till this time if they could have held on.... Coming back is against the rules, when we see signals like that'. To which a juror added, 'They are not born that sort about here'. [67] Within days the press had turned Jimmy's words into 'Caister Men Never Turn Back' and his immortality was assured.

The disaster became national news and thousands flocked to the village on Sunday 17th November, the day of the funeral. Since their recovery the bodies of those lost had lain in the lifeboat shed, all except that of Charles Bonney George, which was not found until April the following year, on the beach at Kessingland, opposite the home of author, H. Rider Haggard. The funeral procession wound its way two abreast, through the streets of Caister, to the spot in the little cemetery that is still so evocative today. The men left behind six widows and 33 dependent children. A public subscription was quickly launched and money poured in, eventually reaching the grand total of £11,870.

The beachmen travelled the country to assist in the fund raising. In February Jimmy was in Luton, telling of his experiences on that town's lifeboat Saturday and in July Jack Haylett was a guest in Leeds where £800 was raised.

Jimmy became something of an overnight celebrity, and on the 6th January 1902, King Edward VII, patron of the R.N.L.I., presented him with the Institution's gold medal at Sandringham House. When the pair met the King is reputed to have said, 'Hello Mr. Haylett', to which Jimmy replied, 'Hello Mr. King'. In their subsequent conversation Jimmy expressed the hope that his Majesty would live to be a hundred and then die and go to heaven. He also told the King, 'There is one thing always gives me courage and that is when I see poor fellows in the rigging of a wreck I always put myself among them and say, 'What would I give if a Life-boat came to save me'.[68]

On the 30th June 1903 a fine memorial to the men who had died was unveiled in the cemetery, a poignant reminder of the selfless bravery of the men who Never Turn Back. But life had to go on. As coxswain Aaron Haylett was one of those lost in the disaster, Charlie Sneller was made temporary coxswain until John Wampo Brown was elected to the post in January 1902. It turned out to be a short-term appointment for in 1903 Aaron's cousin, John Sprat Haylett replaced him. Sprat was asked to advise on a new lifeboat and so he, Charlie Sneller and Paul George, were soon touring other stations to assess the qualities of their boats.

Eventually an order was placed with the Thames Iron Works of Blackwall and on the 23rd July 1903 the *Nancy Lucy* was named at a ceremony at Caister. Her first launch was to the Scottish steam drifter *Shamrock*, stranded on the Patch, off Caister on the 24th October that year. After standing by for three hours the lifeboatmen managed to get her afloat and the accounts record £5.2.4d. boat money.

The most memorable service the *Nancy Lucy* performed was to the Russian barque *Anna Precht*, of Mariehamn, on the 18th September 1906. She had set sail from Borga in Finland with a cargo

61. The 'White' lifeboat store shed, and lifeboat, Caister beach c1930. The shed was erected in 1887.

58

62. Caister Lifeboat Medal Winners, 1906.

Back row, left to right, John Plummer, Frank Clowes (Hon. Secretary), Solomon Brown. Front row, John 'Sprat' Haylett, Jimmy Haylett, Walter 'Sequah' Haylett. Jimmy is wearing his gold medal, the other four their silver medals awarded for rescuing the crew of the *Anna Precht.*

of deals and board ends, bound for the Southgates Road Box factory, at Yarmouth. At the height of a north-easterly gale sweeping the east coast, she drove onto the Barber and almost immediately broke in two. The first indication the Caister men had of what had occurred was when they saw three seamen struggling in the surf. The coastguards pulled them from the water and Station Officer Brattle immediately sent for Sprat, who mustered a crew and with great difficulty launched the *Nancy Lucy.*

The Caister men soon found themselves amidst the vessel's cargo and wreckage, to which the crew were clinging. The master and a lad were spotted lashed to a portion of the vessel's side. Boarding the wreckage the lifeboatmen released them and hauled them into the lifeboat. During the next hour four more of the crew were discovered and rescued and, once another crewman, had been picked up from a steamer anchored in the Roads, the *Nancy Lucy* set sail for Yarmouth harbour.

Recognising the dangerous nature of this service the R.N.L.I. awarded Sprat its silver medal and also gave silver medals to John Plummer, Solomon Brown and Walter Haylett, for jumping onto the wreckage to save those unable to help themselves. A grateful Russian Lifesaving Society also presented them with medals and diplomas.

Between 1900 and the outbreak of the First World War the remaining yawl, *Eclat*, was only mentioned in the accounts in relation to two services, to the s.s. *Bramiam* in 1903 and the s.s. *Givalia* in 1909, the first of these being in conjunction with the lifeboat *Nancy Lucy*. The Beach Company was now, for all intents and purposes, the Lifeboat Company.

Until the 1860s the Caister seafarers made a living from salvaging, 'longshore fishing and working the boats of the Yarmouth deep-sea fisheries, the latter confined to the Spring mackerel and the Autumn herring voyages. These fisheries amounted to three to four months work a year, scarcely enough to make boat owning an attractive proposition, especially as mortgages had to be taken out to purchase them. This all changed with the introduction of trawling.

Trawling from Yarmouth started on a small scale in the 1840s and remained relatively unimportant until 1855-6 when a large number of smacks moved from Barking to the port, most notably Samuel Hewett's Short Blue Fleet. The reason for the move was to reduce costs by being closer to the fishing grounds. The advantage of trawling was that it could be pursued all the year round and by1875 there were 400 trawling smacks working from Yarmouth and Gorleston. It was usual for these smacks to make a six-week voyage, the vessels sailing in fleets under the command of an experienced skipper, who was known as the 'Admiral of the Fleet'. Such a man was Caister's John Brown. Each fleet had in attendance fast sailing cutters to take the catch to the London market. But there were also 'single boaters', i.e. boats that made weekly trips and short voyages. Some of these worked with the fleets, others landed their catches at Yarmouth to be sent by rail to London.

The concept of single boating appealed to the Caister men, but they worked herring luggers, which were significantly different from trawling smacks. The lugger was of slighter build and carried lugsails, for it was only necessary to sail to the fishing grounds, cast the nets, and drift with the tide. The latter were heavier and sported a smack or dandy rig suitable for towing a trawl. The answer was the introduction of what were called 'converter smacks', i.e. boats that could be rigged for both types of fishing. In the late 1860s this innovation, together with the prospect of all the year round fishing, tempted several Caister skippers into boat owning, all of them acquiring newly built smack or dandy rigged boats.

The first to do so were Aaron King, John George, and Jimmy Haylett. In 1867 they pooled their resources to buy a smack, which they called the *Red Jacket* after the Beach Company yawl of that name. Unfortunately, on the 16th April 1869, she was lost in the North Sea and that ended their brief association with smack owning. The Plummer family was next to become involved. In 1868

63. The new Fish Market at Yarmouth, opened in 1867, the year the first Caister fishermen ventured into deep-sea boat owning.

64. Clay Road, looking north c1910. The building on the left, with the staging, was the net warehouse of George Haylett and his sons. The women on the staging are their beatsters. The building in the left foreground was also a net warehouse, run by the Plummer family.

Robert Plummer, his brother William and their father John joined forces to buy the smack *Orion*. The following year Walter Haylett and his brother Joseph, together with Ben Barnard bought a smack, naming her *Eclat*, also after a Beach Company yawl. She was mortgaged to secure £300, which they were soon able to pay off.

With success seemingly assured two more boat owning ventures were established in 1870. Henry James Brown and Henry Brown bought the *Two Sisters*, under a mortgage from fish salesman J.W. De Caux, and a consortium of Thomas Manship, George Hodds, Robert Purdy and Henry Knights bought the *Betsy*, the latter pair being the first 'old' Caister men to become involved.

In December 1870 the Norwich Mercury published a list of the most successful fishing smacks in the recent Home Fishing at Yarmouth. The *Eclat* (125 lasts) was placed second and the *Orion* (108 lasts) sixth. It was a very good year, for 70 lasts was usually reckoned to be a fair return.

In 1871 the census provided a snapshot of these boats at work for on census night, the 2nd April, they were out trawling. The *Orion*, under skipper William Plummer, was working off the Well Bank, the *Eclat*, with Walter Haylett at the helm, was nine miles north-east of Yarmouth and Robert Purdy had the *Betsy* working the Black Bank.

Later that year two of Jimmy Haylett's sons, James and George, together with Robert King and Robert Smith, bought another fishing boat to receive a Beach Company yawl name, the *Zephyr*.

In general terms the 1870s were good years for these men, prompting more skippers to move into boat owning, but one boatowner did not find this satisfying enough. One day in August 1871 William Plummer left the Green Gate tavern, walked slowly down Tan Lane to the beach, took off his clothes and was not heard of again until his decomposed body was washed up on Scratby beach. His share in the *Orion* passed to his father who in 1874 made his other son, Robert, sole owner of the boat. In 1876 Robert sold her to Gorleston man, John Nelson, and bought a new boat, which he called the *William and John*, after his two sons, but in October 1881, she was lost with all hands. In August the following year he replaced her with the *Fairy*, newly built by Critten at his Cobholm yard.

In 1872 Walter Haylett and his partners bought the *Eclipse* under a mortgage to secure £400 from fish salesman John Malden. They followed this, in 1873, with the purchase of an old herring lugger the *James and Ellen*, the boat which in 1867 had capsized the Gorleston Ranger Company's lifeboat *Rescuer* with the loss of 25 lives, including six boatmen. The following year they sold the *Eclipse*.

This partnership was dissolved in 1877 with Ben Barnard taking the *Eclat* and Walter Haylett the *James and Ellen*. Later that year the other partner, Joseph Haylett, bought a boat, which he named after his two sons, the *Joseph and William*. Two years later Walter teamed up with one of his skippers, Robert Green, to buy the *Zephyr*, sold to them by fish salesman Horatio Fenner, after Robert King had defaulted on his mortgage.

In 1875 Henry Brown sold his half of the *Two Sisters* to Henry James Brown, but in 1877 she was another Caister boat to be lost with all hands in the North Sea. He promptly replaced her with the *Two Friends*, also bought from Henry Brown, who was described as of California at the time.

The Thomas Manship partnership bought the *Vigilant* in 1873, but in 1875 they also parted company. Manship and Knights took the *Vigilant*, while Purdy had the *Betsy*. In 1876, the other partner, George Hodds, started afresh with the *Shade of Evening*.

The Haylett brothers and their partners bought their second boat, the *Harmony*, in 1873, but in 1876 they too split up, leaving the Hayletts with the boat, which the following year was also lost with all hands. By 1877 Robert King was sole owner of the *Zephyr*, but as has already been noted

65. The Gorleston Lifeboat *Rescuer* being capsized by the fishing lugger *James and Ellen* in the entrance to Yarmouth harbour, 1867. The lugger was bought by Walter Haylett and partners in 1873 and fished by them until 1892.

62

66. The fishing smack *Speranza*, YH 382, built by Reynolds of Lowestoft for Robert Leech Plummer, in 1893. The Plummer family fished her until 1911. She is shown after her completion at Beeching's Yarmouth yard.

he lost her when he defaulted on his mortgage. That same year the Haylett brothers bought the *Seamew*.

In 1877 a new group comprising Joseph Sutton, James King and John Bishop Manship was formed to buy an old lugger called the *Eustace*. Early in 1878 Manship left this partnership to go it alone with the *Edith and Annie* and shortly afterwards the *Eustace* was lost off Yarmouth. In 1879 Joseph Sutton bought an old lugger, the *Cormorant*, and James King acquired the *Sparkling Foam*.

The last of the new owners to throw their sou'westers into the ring in the 1870s was Solomon Brown, who had recently moved from California, and his son William. In 1879 they bought a boat, which they called the *Solomon*.

By the end of the decade there were 18 Caister boatowners, owning between them 14 fishing smacks. Most of these men were successful skippers who wanted a greater share in the money earned by their skill and endeavour. They were of the opinion that all the year round fishing would pay off the mortgages on these boats, with a tidy sum left over, but skill was not enough to secure success in the fishing business, for that elusive commodity depended on a number of factors.

As far as the herring and mackerel fisheries were concerned, supply and demand had to be in balance if a steady income was to be made. A glut would ruin the price and too few fish would mean high prices, but a lower overall take. The quality of the fish was also important and bad weather was a mixed blessing, for while it would limit the number of boats that went out, it could also damage the gear or cause it to be lost altogether, which would prove costly. Fluctuations in demand would also affect the final outcome.

Throughout the 1870s the returns from these fisheries were reasonable enough, but at the end of the decade, and throughout the 1880s, there were many poor seasons, with boat owners scarcely

67. The fishing smack *Paradox,* YH 951, entering Yarmouth Harbour c1900. She was built by Richards of Lowestoft in 1884 for Walter Haylett and fished by him until 1909, when she was broken up. According to Harry George she, 'would go like a train'.

covering their costs, let alone being able to pay off their mortgages and take money home. At the same time the Yarmouth trawl fishery went into terminal decline as the grounds within easy reach became fished out, the railway companies favoured Lowestoft, and a major competitor, Grimsby, went over to steam trawlers. These events resulted in a disastrous period for the Caister boat owners and whilst a few managed to weather the storm many others went out of business.

Robert Plummer was one of the fortunate ones. He kept the *Fairy* afloat and in 1893 even managed to expand his business with the purchase of the *Speranza,* but in 1896 he died leaving both smacks to his widow, Susannah, and her brothers, master mariner Aaron Bonney George and Dennis George, a retired fish salesman. Remarkably both boats survived well into the age of steam drifting.

In similar vein Walter Haylett survived. In 1884 he sold his share in the *Zephyr* to his partner, Robert Green and bought the *Paradox.* According to Harry George she was in a class of her own, and 'would go like a train'. In 1885 Walter mortgaged her to Horatio Fenner, but managed to keep up the payments. He also mortgaged the *James and Ellen* to Fenner in 1886, and kept hold of her until 1892, when she was sold to Norwegian owners.

Walter's relationship with Fenner seems to have been a good one for in 1891 the fish salesman sold him the *Thalia,* which he owned in partnership with two of his sons, Walter and Ambrose, the latter a dockgate keeper in London. Fenner provided the finance. In 1887 Robert Green sold the *Zephyr* to Thomas and William Pumfrey.

Of the other Caister boat owners in the age of sail, Ben Barnard died in 1883 in possession of the *Eclat.* By then he was living in Southtown and his widow, Emma, ran the boat until her

64

bankruptcy in 1886. In 1885 Robert Purdy had the Betsy taken away from him when he defaulted on his mortgage. That year the *Zephyr II* disaster removed four other boat owners. George Hodds had mortgaged the *Shade of Evening* in 1881 to Edgar Rushmer. Following his drowning Rushmer quickly sold her to recoup his money. Hannah King, the widow of James ran the *Sparkling Foam* for a few years then she too had to pack up. In 1884 Joseph Sutton had bought the *Nell* from James Sharman and mortgaged her to fish salesman, George Giles. Six months after Joseph's death Giles sold her to Harry Horne.

Joseph Haylett's widow, Eleanor, managed to run the *Joseph and William* until 1889, when the boat was also taken away by Giles, the circumstances of which show how fraught these occasions could be. No sooner had the *Joseph and William* docked, on the 9th December, than Giles seized the boat, nets and everything else on board. Eleanor, who had by then become Mrs Manning, removed the nets from the Denes, on the advice of her solicitor, Frank Clowes, and took them to a warehouse in Caister. As a result Giles went to the police and reported them stolen. Eleanor was taken to court for stealing the nets, but was found not guilty, the nets having been purchased out of her own capital, not the borrowed money. Contending that she had lost money and reputation she in turn took Giles to court in an action to 'recover damages for malicious imprisonment'. Giles won, but was unable to recover his costs for by then she had become a bankrupt on her own petition, her assets being at the time £154.2s. and her liabilities £456.17s.6d.

Other failures followed. In 1887 John Bishop Manship had to give up the *Edith and Annie*. Trying to buck the trend Henry Knights bought the *Ionia* in 1885 and mortgaged her to Norford Suffling, but four years later he lost her after she was driven ashore while making for the harbour.

68. The fishing smack *Shade of Evening*, YH 676, in Yarmouth harbour. Built at Gorleston in 1866 she was bought in 1876 by George Benjamin Hodds. George was lost in the *Zephyr II* disaster in 1885, whereupon his mortgagee, fish salesman Edgar Rushmer, sold the boat.

The crew of nine were saved by the Gorleston rocket crew and she was salvaged for £45. Not long after this Suffling sold her to John Neave.

In 1890 David Saunders bought the *Welcome*, but could not keep up with the repayments, losing her in 1894. In 1893 Jimmy Haylett's son, James, bought the *Masterpiece*, but a few years later he too was sold up, also losing the *Seamew*.

James's brother George was more fortunate. In 1882 the pair bought the newly built *Ithuriel*. After ten years George acquired his bother's share and successfully fished her until 1902. In 1893 he bought the *Ambrosia*. That same year Robert Puddens Brown bought the *Gertrude*. He died in 1901 and his widow, Sarah sold her to Jimmy Pitchers Junior, of Yarmouth. In 1894 Henry James Brown had the *Two Friends* taken away for the usual reason.

Perhaps the most unlucky ownership in this period was that of Solomon Gundy Brown and his son William. Following their purchase of the *Solomon* in 1881 they bought the *William*. In 1884 the *Solomon* was wrecked on Scroby. She was replaced by the *Venus*, which in turn was lost in a gale with many other smacks in 1889 together with her skipper, Solomon's eldest son, Solomon Wright (Brown). This gale left seven Caister women widowed. By then Solomon had already lost his son Dennis in the smack *Enos*, in 1878. As if this was not enough the *William* was stranded on the Barber in 1899 and, whilst the crew was rescued by the lifeboat *Beauchamp*, the smack itself became a total wreck. Ironically the *William's* owner, William Brown, was in the lifeboat and his brother Charles was at the helm of the smack. By then their father, Solomon had died, from injuries received during a lifeboat service to the full rigged ship *Soudan*, in 1897.

Of Solomon Brown Harry Boash George wrote, 'The last old-time skipper I saw in 'uniform',

69. Solomon 'Gundy' Brown 1831-1897. Fishing boat owner, beachman and lifeboat-man.

70. Solomon Wright (Brown) 1850-1889. Lost in the smack *Venus*.

71. The steam drifter *Cicero* YH 177, entering Yarmouth harbour c1910. Built at Lowestoft in 1903 for John and William Plummer she was one of the earliest steam drifters to be Caister owned. The Plummers fished her until she was sold to French owners in 1920.

that is top hat, walking stick and blue guernsey and trousers, was Old Solly Brown. Each Sunday morning Solly would go to the House of God dressed like that'. Harry himself started in sail, buying the old smack *Harry* in 1906 before selling her six months later.

By the mid-1890s only three Caister fishing businesses had managed to survive the bad days, those of Robert Plummer and his son John, Walter Haylett and his son Edwin, and George Haylett. All were nicely placed to take advantage of the introduction of steam technology to the Yarmouth fishing fleet and the exceptional boom years that were to follow.

Credit is usually given to the Fenner brothers, Horatio and Ernest for introducing the steam drifter to Yarmouth, when in 1895 they brought to the port the *Salamander* and the *Puffin*, but Caister's Walter Haylett fished with steam before them, as recounted by Charles Green. 'It was he (Walter), indeed, who first used a steam-vessel for "drifting". About 1890, he chartered a small trawler, the Edith of Leith, as a trial venture, one so successful that it led to the general introduction of steam-drifters'.[69]

Reporting on the herring fishing in 1898 G. H. Harris wrote, 'The year 1898 may be taken, too, as signalising the advent of the steam drifter, which must be carefully distinguished, of course, from the steam trawler. Steam drifters are not a novelty, but their muster has been too small to exercise an appreciable influence in the trade, This year they numbered twenty, and can no longer be reckoned a negligible quantity. Probably they are destined to extirpate the sailing lugger...'.[70] He went on to say that, 'It would not pay to build a steamer that could follow her business for three months only to lay up on the "hard" for the rest of the year, as the old luggers did. But if a plan can be found whereby she can drift for the better part of the year, she may pay. And apparently, in the development of the West Coast and Irish fishings, such a place has been found'.

The following year was reckoned at the time, to be the best year ever. Exported barrels of

72. The steam drifter *Paradox II,* YH 710, leaving Yarmouth harbour, c1925. Built in Yarmouth in 1910 for Walter Haylett and his son Edwin, she was given the name of their well-known sailing smack, which had recently been broken up. In 1920 Edwin sold her to the Plummer brothers. She was broken up in 1929.

herring increased from 45,872 to 141,585, chiefly to Russia and Germany. It was the start of an unprecedented period of success for the herring industry, with improvement year on year, culminating in the spectacular season of 1913.

In July 1899 William Hilton Brown bought the old Thurso built boat *Alpha*, thereby becoming the first Caister man to own a steam drifter. It was fated to be a short-lived venture for Hilton was drowned in the *Beauchamp* disaster and the boat was quickly sold to Simon Holmes of Yarmouth. His brother, Robert Puddens Brown, followed him into steam, buying the *Lily* in 1900.

That same year George Haylett took possession of the newly built steam drifter *Grace Darling*. Unfortunately, in September 1911, she was sunk off Scarborough, struck by the steamer *Seamew*, the steel bow of the larger vessel easily cutting into the wooden hull of the drifter. In 1904 he bought the *Diadem*, transferring a third share in both boats to his son, Fred, in 1906, having sold the smack *Ambrosia*. In February 1911 he transferred a further third to Fred and the remaining third to another son, Ernest before, at the age of 64, retiring from the herring fishing business. Later that year his sons bought the *GMH*, named after Ernest's young son, Gordon Meredith. George was the only one of Jimmy Haylett's sons to live to old age. He was a survivor of the *Zephyr II* disaster, which took his brother Fred, and his other brothers, James and Aaron, were lost in the *Beauchamp* disaster.

In 1902 Walter Haylett bought the *Boadicea*, taking in with him his sons Walter and Edwin, before selling the sailing smack *Thalia*. Walter Junior soon left the partnership and in 1908 Walter and Edwin reverted to sail when they bought the ketch rigged *Prosperity*. In 1910 they invested in another steam drifter, which they called the *Paradox II*, as their smack of that name had recently been broken up. The *Prosperity* was sold to Norwegian owners in 1911.

The last of the surviving boatowners from the age of sail, the Plummer family went into steam in 1903. After his father's death in 1896, John had managed the two family owned sailing smacks, but in 1903 the *Fairy* was sold and John, together with his brother William, a marine engineer, bought the steam drifter *Cicero*. In 1908, together with another brother, Robert, they bought the *Goodhope* and in 1911, after selling their sailing smack, *Speranza*, to be broken up, they bought a new drifter, which was given her name.

In 1907, after selling the sailing smack *Harry*, Boash George bought the drifters *Osprey* and *Pleiades*, the latter in partnership with two Scottish men. Selling the former in 1909 and the latter in 1911, he bought the *Archimedes*. In 1912 he acquired the *Frons Olivae*, and in 1913 the *Kitty George* before making his final pre- First World War purchase, the *Caister Castle*, in July 1914.

John Clinker Brown, the son of Robert Brown, the owner of the sailing smack *Gertrude*, teamed up with John Chase in 1909 to buy the *Boy Billy* and in 1912 they also purchased the *Covent Garden*, named after the lifeboat of that name.

In 1902 Commander James Bloomfield arrived in Yarmouth to work for the Smith's Dock Trust

73. The four-masted ship *Nile,* of Glasgow, a 'big boat'. In October 1890 she was refloated from the Cross Sand by the crews of the lifeboats *Covent Garden* and *Godsend,* together with a number of steam tugs. £80 boat money was entered in the Company accounts. As the Norwegian ship *Thor II* of Sandijford, she was sunk in the Atlantic by a U-boat in July 1917.

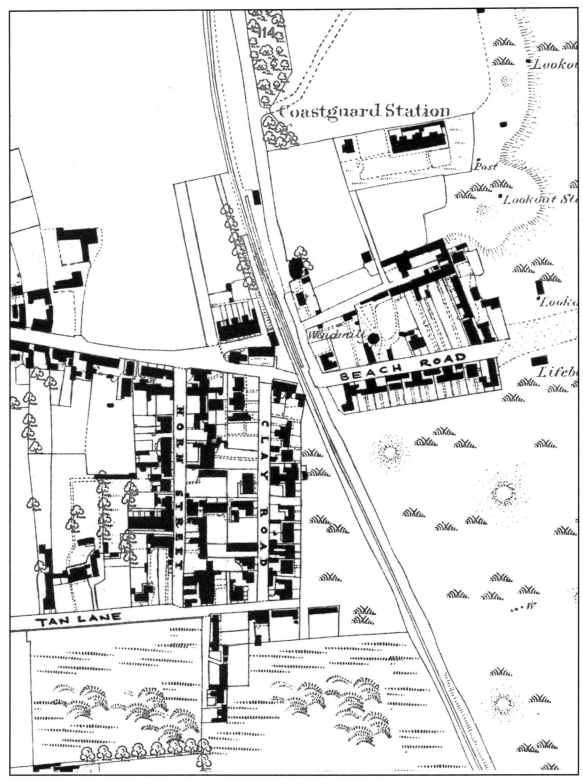

74. The fully developed Caister Beach Village as it appeared in 1885.

Company Ltd., and in 1911 he formed his own fishing company. Bloomfield had a knack of employing the best skippers and he retained their services by taking them in as co-partners. One such man was George Wildawn Green, who in 1912 took a quarter share in the newly built *Ocean Retriever*. In 1914 he bought the rest and owned the boat in the name of a company, George W Green Ltd. Jack Hubbard was another Caister man who went into partnership with Bloomfields on a similar basis, with the *Ocean Treasure*. Both these boats were run from Yarmouth.

The other Caister man to take up steam drifter owning before the First World War was James Shinny Powley, who in 1912 took a half share in the *JS*, with Richard Sutton. In 1916 he bought the *Piscatorial* in partnership with Harry Eastick.

Deep-sea fishing took the Caister men around the British Isles, but it was not unusual for them to mix that pursuit with what was termed 'big boating', that is working as merchant seaman. This took them round the world. Robert Plummer was a seaman in sailing ships. When he arrived in Australia he jumped ship to try his hand in the gold fields before returning to Caister to become a fishing boat owner. Others such as, John Sneller, Aaron George and Jonathan Purdy became masters of merchant vessels, being men who commanded respect when they retired to the village. Capt. Purdy became the first chairman of the Parish Council in 1894.

Aaron's nephew, Paul George, was a man who moved from fishing into the merchant service. He started as a boy cook on his father's sailing smack, in 1893, and by 1899 was experienced enough to be offered a skipper's berth in a new steam drifter, but he decided to enter the merchant service instead, joining a tramp steamer as an able seaman. Over the next 15 years he voyaged in sail and steam around the world steadily gaining promotion until in June 1914 he was given his first command. During the First World War he had eight run ins with submarines and fought two actions, for the latter of which he received the D.S.C and Lloyds silver medal. After the war he continued as a merchant ship captain, largely for the Thompson Steamship Company, before retiring after 48 years at sea.

In the last 40 years of the 19th century Caister did not experience the rapid population growth of the previous decades, but by 1901 another 400 people had been added to the parish figure and a similar increase occurred in the next 15 years. Not all this increase, related to seafaring activity, but the beach village became more densely developed and a new area of housing on the Yarmouth Road became home to an influx of migrant fishermen, largely from inland Flegg.

The deep-sea boat owners were responsible for much of the new development in the beach village. In the 1870s, when business was profitable, several of these men had new houses built there, including Walter Haylett, George Haylett, James Haylett Junior, and Henry Knights. Manship's property fronted Beach Road and was called Ivy House. A Mrs. Symonds later bought it and, on her death it was acquired by the Reverend Robson, who covered the forecourt with a large room and turned the whole building into an Institute.

Prior to the upsurge of deep sea boat owning in the 1870s the Caister owned boats were run from Yarmouth, but the new owners could see cost and family advantages in working from home and this produced a rash of buildings called net warehouses. These two storey structures were approximately 45 feet long by 15 feet wide and were usually orientated with one long side facing south, to maximise the amount of daylight in the upper or beating chamber, enabling women called 'beatsters', to mend the spoiled nets in good light. The ground floor of these buildings was where the gear was stored and maintained by men called 'ransackers', who also distributed the nets to the beatsters.[71]

There were at least 13 warehouses in the village, most of them clustered in and around the beach

75. Yarmouth Road c1900. The area was in effect a new 'suburb' started in the late 1860s. It was popular with Flegg born fishermen working the all the year round Yarmouth fishery.

village, near to where the owners and their beatsters, often family members, lived. Only one was built off the Yarmouth Road, the obvious place to site them in relation to the transportation of nets to and from Yarmouth.

Associated with some of these establishments were tanning coppers, in which the mended nets were steeped in the preservative cutch. At the Plummer chamber, at the northern end of Victoria Street, there was a tanning copper, but also some vats. These were square concrete tanks, in which a whole fleet of nets could be treated. The nets were placed in them to soak over-night. They would be covered with boards, weighted down by pig iron ballast, from the old sailing smacks. In the morning the tanks would be drained and, the nets left an hour before being spread on the dunes to dry. Most of the warehouses survive, but they are scarcely recognisable in their current use as houses.

The other fishing related structures to appear in the beach village and elsewhere were small smokehouses. When the fishermen came home they would bring with them herring to be smoked. This provided plenty of work for the smoke house owners, who would also buy herring in Yarmouth for this purpose. This industry was very much village scale, it not being able to cope with the quantity of fish caught by the 'longshoremen, which invariably was sent to Yarmouth. These smokehouses are easily recognised by the small wicket openings in the upper gables. These would be closed during the curing process and opened to let the smoke out when the curing was complete. Harry Mann was a well-known Caister fish curer, with a smoke house to the rear of 57 Tan Lane. He kept a horse and cart and would hawk the cured fish around the adjacent villages.

The only significant extension to the beach village took place at the seaward end of Beach Road. The Common bordered the south side, but in the late 1860s / early 1870s John Clowes sold frontage plots to a number of individuals, enabling a row of south facing houses to be built. As part of this process Jimmy Haylett bought a plot in September 1869. On this he built what is now 101 Beach

Road, moving there in 1870 from his small cottage, facing the beach. The plot to the east had recently been sold to Tom Pout George, and that to the west to Jimmy's brother-in-law, Aaron King.

At the western end was a warehouse built by George Haylett and Robert Smith to work the smack *Zephyr*. The Haylett family used it until Gordon Goee Haylett finished with the fishing in 1961.

On the northern side of this part of Beach Road stood the East Windmill until its demolition in 1905. The reclaimed bricks were used to build part of the terrace of houses on the site.

In 1877 the Yarmouth & Stalham Light Railway Company opened a line from Yarmouth to Ormesby. Passing through Caister, this effectively cut off the main part of the beach village from the seaward extension and the beach. Until then some of the coastguards had been accommodated in a row of cottages on Beach Road, at the northern end of Clay Road. Alongside these stood the shed, which housed the Board of Trade life saving apparatus, operated by the coastguards. This severance prompted the building, in 1881, of a terrace of coastguard houses and a house for the Chief Officer, much closer to the sea, to the north of Beach Road. Near them stood a lookout and the post to practice the use of the rocket line. Their old accommodation is now called Railway Cottages.

Until the late 1860s there was little development associated with Yarmouth Road, but thereafter a new suburb of the village was built, largely comprising terrace houses, the dated examples of which range from 1869 to 1908. This area had no real relationship with the sea at Caister, but it became popular with the Flegg born fishermen working in the all the year round Yarmouth fishing industry. The 1881 Census revealed 20 such men and their families, living in these terraces, and

76. 'Beachman's Village and Lifeboat Station', from a drawing by C.J. Staniland, 1885. The Beach Company watchhouse and lookout stand in front of the East Windmill. The yawl in the foreground is the *Red Jacket*.

73

77. Beach Road, Caister c1920.

this figure steadily grew as the area expanded.

Down on the beach very little changed in these years other than the already noted relocation of the coastguards. The Beach Company property was maintained and replaced when the need arose, and that most vulnerable of structures, the lookout was rebuilt in 1889. In 1885 Charles Staniland described the company shed in the following terms, 'The shed is in the upper story a watch-house and beachmen's parliament house, where the affairs of the nation (of Caister beachmen) are discussed, accounts settled, and business transacted; following up the parallel by even (like other legislators) taking long and comfortable snoozes on the benches which run round the building. One side contains a bay window, from which through sliding shutters a view can be obtained north, east or south, and where some beachman is always on watch. Two men are on watch every night and all night, taken by rotation from the company, the list hanging up in the shed. Under the shed is a carpenter's shop, where the renowned James Vincent manufactures oars, masts, etc, etc., for the company, and even condescends to goodwives washing tubs and other domestic appliances'.[72]

With so many men in one place with the same forename and surname, it was necessary to devise a way of distinguishing them, one from another. The answer was for everyone to have a unique nickname. Once given to an individual, the nickname would, often as not, be passed down, and would, for all intents and purposes, replace the surname.

These nicknames survive in oral tradition from the mid-19th century, but their meanings have usually been lost. This is not surprising when one considers the nickname 'Skipper' that John Woodhouse acquired. On the face of it one could be forgiven for thinking he was, or had been, a skipper of deep-sea fishing boats, but this was not the case. As a young boy his uncle had given him a sailor's cap, which had come from a rescued seaman. It had the name 'skipjack' on the ribbon and because he wore it all the time he was soon being called 'Skipper' and the nickname stuck.

5. 1914 – 1939

The Home Fishing of 1913 turned out to be the best ever. In simple terms 825,000,000 herrings were caught by 999 drifters, grossing £1,000,000. Fishermen, owners, buyers and curers all had a good season and the boats were packed so tightly in the harbour that it was possible to walk across them from bank to bank. Then came the First World War and the herring fishing was never to be the same again.

The war officially started on the 4th August 1914, but long before then its inevitability was obvious and preparations had been made to augment the Navy. On the 28th July the coastguard were called up and in early August the men of the Royal Naval Reserve (RNR) were told to report. This organisation was established in 1859 to recruit men from amongst the merchant marine and fishermen, who could be called up in the event of war. At the outset each recruit received a month's paid training and a retainer thereafter.

Attracted by the pay and the uniform many Caister seafarers enrolled and were subsequently called up, some entering the regular Navy, but most joining what would later be termed the Patrol Service. There was also another reservist organisation, the Royal Naval Volunteer Reserve (RNVR) and some Caister men entered the senior service via this route.

The Patrol Service was something of a navy within a navy as it consisted of requisitioned trawlers and drifters, crewed largely by the fishermen of the RNR. As far as trawlers were concerned they tended to be taken with their crews and deployed on decoy duties, mine-sweeping and submarine chasing. The drifters did not have such a close relationship with their own skippers and

78. Proud RNR relatives, c1914.

Seated, left to right; Joe 'Roper' George (Skipper RN), —— (Skipper RN). Back row, Tom Nichols, Tom Nichols senior, Alfred 'Sticks' Hubbard.

79. Jack Hubbard in the uniform of a Skipper RN, c1914. He was a survivor of the *Beauchamp* disaster of 1901 and was briefly the part owner with Bloomfields of the steam drifter *Ocean Treasure*, YH 574.

80. Frank Brown, boy cook, on the RN Drifter *Roburn* when, on the 19th October 1916, she was sunk by German destroyers in the Straits of Dover. Frank became a POW.

81. Bertie 'Geesha' George, left, and Robert 'Boash' George, right, on RNR training c1900. In the First World War 'Boash' won the DSC, whereas 'Geesha' was killed.

crews and were mostly used for harbour work. Each harbour had two such boats, on board one of which was a naval lieutenant who would be ferried out to new arrivals to check their papers. If the papers were in order the vessel was given the appropriate signal flags and allowed to proceed to the docks.

The pick of the Yarmouth drifter fleet was employed in this way, leaving only the older steam drifters and some newly built ones to continue to fish throughout the war, largely for home consumption, as the overseas markets were no longer accessible.

Most of the Caister boats were requisitioned, their owners receiving around £55 a month from the Government for their hire, and the RNR Caister men were posted to vessels around the British Isles and further afield. Those with skipper's tickets were given the rank of Skipper RN, and placed in charge of requisitioned fishing boats, some were designated Chief Skipper and given more responsibility. In this capacity Joe Roper George was placed in charge of a dozen drifters based at Kingstown in Ireland and shared in the sinking of at least one German U-boat.

Not so fortunate was Ben Titabee Haylett, skipper of H.M. Drifter *Roburn*. On the night of 29th October 1916 German destroyers raided the Straits of Dover and sank six drifters and two destroyers of the Dover Patrol. Titabee together with three other Caister men, the mate, Ted Virgin Brown, the driver, Ernie Haylett, and the cook Frank Brown were captured. Young Frank was separated from the rest because he was wounded and spent nine months in German occupied Bruges. He was reported dead and a memorial service was held for him in the parish church.

Robert Aaron George was skipper of the drifter *Lottie Leask*, in the Adriatic, when in 1915 a German cruiser sank a number of drifters off Brindisi. His was last in the line and managed to survive as the cruiser was chased off by Italian destroyers. He rescued a large number of people from a sinking vessel for which he was awarded the Distinguished Service Cross (DSC).

The Caister owned or part owned Ocean boats, the *Retriever* and the *Treasure*, were requisitioned in September 1914. Both were fitted with 6 pounder guns and employed on patrol duties.

To the fishermen, being able to wear a naval uniform made them feel special and they could not wait to visit the photographer in their designated port to have the fact recorded for their relations back home. As a result many such photographs are to be found in local collections.

Three Caister owned boats succumbed to the rigours of the war, the *Frons Olivae* struck a mine on the 28th October 1915, the *Boadicea* was lost on the 8th January 1917 and the *Piscatorial* was sunk on the 29th December the same year.

But loss of property is nothing compared to loss of life and the village war memorial in the church records the names of 48 men who gave their lives in the First World War. Many of these served at sea, such as Alonzo Strowger, who was lost when HM Drifter *Cloverbank* struck a mine on the 24th April 1916 and Charles Brown who died in similar circumstances on the 20th October 1917 whilst aboard HM Trawler *Stratten*. Others such as Bertie Geesha George, perished in the Senior Service, when HMS *Hogue* was torpedoed on the 29th September 1914 and Edward Robson, brother of the Rector, was Chaplin aboard HMS *Aboukir* when she too was sunk by a U-boat on the 22nd September 1914.

While the men were away German warships shelled the village, in September 1914 and again in April 1916. Fortunately on the first occasion the shells exploded at sea and on the second, while the shells fell in the village, they caused no damage to life or property.

Once the war was over the Admiralty no longer needed the requisitioned drifters and the surviving Caister boats were returned to their owners. Four years had taken its toll on the herring fishery and the seas were still mined. The pre-war boat owners had to decide whether they wanted to resume fishing, given that many had made good money in the decade before the war and had

82. The steam drifter *Frans Olivae,* YH 217, heading towards the harbour's mouth, Yarmouth, c1914. Built for Harry 'Boash' George in 1912, she struck a mine in the North Sea on 12th October 1915 and was totally lost.

83. The steam drifter *Goodhope,* YH736, entering Yarmouth harbour, c1910. Built in 1902, she was bought by the Plummer brothers in 1908, but not fished after the First World War. She was sold in 1920 to a Liverpool owner.

also been well paid for the use of their boats during the war. In the event most of the owners sent their boats to sea again, but of course fishing was in their blood.

The fishermen and boatowners probably assumed that the pre-war boom years would return, but the war had all but destroyed the most important requirement of a successful herring fishery and that was demand for the fish. In 1928 the editor of the Transactions of the Norfolk and Norwich Naturalists Society wrote, 'The success of the Yarmouth herring fishing depends, in the last analysis, upon the capacity of the European peasant to consume salted herrings during the winter. It is not a question of organising a fleet and equipping it to catch herrings, but entirely a matters of marketing the catch, for 95 per cent of the fish landed has to find a foreign destination'.[73]

The main pre-war markets had been Germany, which was now too impoverished to buy the fish and Russia, which, being in the throes of revolution, was largely inaccessible. Add to this foreign competition and the usual variables of damaged gear, gluts and poor quality fish, then it can be readily appreciated that the 1920s was not a good time to be herring fishing. Circumstances did improve, as markets became re-established, and this did encourage the ever-optimistic boat owners to expand their businesses and the more ambitious skippers to venture into boat owning. Only the 1921, 1925, and 1928 seasons were really bad and although the fleet was steadily ageing, new drifters were being built.

John Plummer and his sleeping partners, William and Robert, reclaimed the *Goodhope, Cicero* and *Speranza,* but they decided not to fish the *Goodhope* again, selling her in July 1920 to a Liverpool owner. After buying the *Paradox II* from Edwin Haylett they also sold the *Cicero,* to a Frenchman. By 1928, John had decided to retire from the business, leaving things in the capable hands of his son Jack.

Walter Haylett had retired from active fishing in 1916, selling the *Paradox II* to his son Edwin.

In 1917 Edwin bought the newly built *Phyllis Mary*, but for some reason, in 1920 sold half to James Moore, a Yarmouth owner and the following year sold him the other half. Finally he bought the *EBC* and fished her until 1926, when he was forced to sell to two Winterton men, bringing to a close the fishing business established by his father nearly 60 years earlier.

Fred Haylett and his brother, Ernest Tready, resumed fishing with the *GMH* and the *Diadem*, both financed by their father George. They also fished the *Animate*, which had been bought in 1917 and the *Berry Castle*, which Fred had acquired for himself in 1918. In February 1921 Fred sold this boat and in 1925 they sold the *GMH* to Henry Catchpole, of Lowestoft. Earlier that year they had also bought the *Animation*. By the late 1920s the old *Diadem* was becoming unseaworthy and was sent to the breakers yard.

The Caister boatowner who had the most spectacular rise and fall was Harry Boash George. Harry had skippered for the Smith's Dock Trust Company before going into boat owning before the war. At the start of hostilities he owned four boats, the *Archimedes, Caister Castle, Frons Olivae* and *Kitty George* all financed by mortgages from boat builder Fellows and Co., or fish salesman Norford Suffling.

He lost the *Frons Olivae* to enemy action in 1915, but from then added eleven boats to his rapidly growing fleet. These were the *Adele* (1915), *Mon Ami* and *Frons Olivae* (1916), *Fancy* (1917), *Herring Gull, La Mascot* and *Innergellie* (1918), *Norford Suffling, Sanscrit, Olivae* and *Sunbeam II* (1919), all financed by the National Provincial Bank.

A few of these he sold during the war, but by the end of 1918 he still owned a substantial fleet,

84. Net Warehouse in Honeymoon Loke, Caister. Walter Haylett and his family originally used it. At the far end is the tanning copper. Much altered, it survives today as a private house.

85. The steam drifter *Kitty George,* YH 263. Built by Fellows of Yarmouth in 1913 for Harry 'Boash' George. He had to sell her in 1919.

some of which had been hired by the Government, whilst others had been fishing. This was Harry's problem. After the war owners of working fishing boats had to pay what was called excess profit-tax. This was assessed on the profit made by the owner in his best year before the war e.g. if the earnings for 1913 were £1,000, but during the war £2,000, then 80% tax was paid on the difference. This measure broke many owners, seemingly hitting Harry hard too.

In January 1919 he sold the *Kitty George, Caister Castle, Mon Ami, Herring Gull, La Mascot, Norford Suffling* and the *Sunbeam II*, and a year later, following the Home Fishing, the *Frons Olivae, Innergellie, Sanscrit* and *Olivae,* managing to pay off the mortgages on all of them.

For three years Harry licked his wounds, but in February 1923 he entered the fray again, this time buying a trawler from an Isle of Man owner, the Scottish boat *Ralph Hall Caine,* also financed by the National Provincial Bank. He then went further and bought a small coaster, but this proved to be his undoing and in 1925 he lost everything.

In later life Harry skippered pleasure boats and made important contributions to Edgar March's books, Sailing Drifters and Sailing Trawlers. His obituary added that he was a champion of new ideas and in 1920 had patented a trawl net.

After the war the widow of Robert Puddens Brown continued to fish the *Lily* but she died in 1921 and the old boat was sold to Albert Tuck. John Clinker Brown and his partner, John Chase, continued to fish, but in 1923 they sold the *Boy Billy* and in 1928, after selling their remaining boat, the *Covent Garden,* they too called it a day.

In April 1918 Shinny Powley sold the *JS* to Harry George, having bought the *Ellen and Irene* from Jack Starchy George of Winterton. He fished her for little more than a year, before selling her to Donald Macleod of Stornaway. In 1920 he went into partnership with Harry Eastick to buy the *Kitty*, but in 1923 the boat was sold to a Sunderland firm and Shinny, like the others, felt it was time to finish with boat owning.

Just before the war ended Jack Hubbard sold his share in the *Ocean Treasure* to the majority shareholder, Bloomfields. Wildawn Green continued with the *Ocean Retriever*, but in 1925 sold the *Ocean Retriever II* (bought 1914), and the *Ocean Dawn* (bought 1919), also to Bloomfields. Things were clearly difficult for him for in January 1926 he transferred ownership of his house, 101 Beach Road, which Jimmy Haylett had had built, to his wife, no doubt as a hedge against losing it if he was declared bankrupt.

At the beginning of the 1930s only three Caister boat ownerships remained, fishing between them five steam drifters. Apart from Harry George those owners who had left the business had not been forced to do so, but some had to settle sizeable debts.

The 1931 Home Fishing was considered to be the worst in living memory. Curers the previous year had lost heavily so they set about finding ways to avoid the same thing happening again. They shortened the season and as a result the overall catch was much smaller, yet prices were no more that half those of 1930. Commentators made the point that since the war the Yarmouth herring fishery had been dogged by dwindling catches and shrinking exports. To this was added the problem of tariffs and quotas, which had recently been introduced by some European Countries.

Things did not improve until 1936 when the season was reckoned to be the best since 1930, although for the boat owners heavy gales, particularly in November, caused considerable damage to gear and the loss of two boats. Regulations were imposed to prevent a glut and these ensured that the price of herring was well maintained. Foreign demand was also better. But it was a false

86. The steam drifter *Ocean Dawn*, YH 47. Built in Aberdeen in 1919 she was bought by Wildawn's company, George W. Green Ltd. In 1925 he sold her to Bloomfields.

87. A group of Bloomfield's skippers, on the South Denes, Yarmouth in the 1920s. Several of them were Caister men or of Caister origin. These are marked with a 'c'.

Back row, left to right; Alfred Peek, Edwin Haylett (c), Dick Brown (c), Ben 'Titabee' Haylett (c), William 'Blucher' Knights, Philip Smith (c), Robert Fuller, Alf Blowers, Moses Rump (c). Front row; Leander 'Jay' George (c), Ezie Smith (c), Alf Tubby, Joe 'Roper' George (c), Charlie Smith (c).

dawn for 1937 was not nearly so good and 1938 was really bad in terms of quality, size of catch and price.

After the Home Fishing of 1932 Wildawn Green had had enough, selling the *Ocean Retriever* to the Balls brothers of Yarmouth. He died two months later. Jack Plummer managed to run the *Speranza* through to the War, although in May 1939 he sold the *Paradox II* to be broken up.

The Haylett brothers, Fred and Ernest Tready, fished the *Animate* through to the war, although Fred sold his controlling share to his brother in 1937. They also continued with the *Animation*, taking in George Woolston as a partner in 1926. By 1936 Woolston owned all the boat. He also managed to survive. Against the general trend the brothers even expanded the business, in 1932 buying the *Rose* with Fred's son George as a partner. In 1937 George acquired the whole of the boat and in 1939 bought the *George Albert*.

The last, wholly new, boat owner to fish in the inter-war period was Albert Crabby Hudson. In 1931, with finance from Richard Sutton, Crabby bought the *A Rose* and in 1938, with finance from Suffling, the *Achievable*, which George and Henry Woodhouse of Winterton had owned, until they defaulted on their mortgage.

But how fared the men who crewed the boats in these difficult times? Being share fishermen there was no unemployment pay and therefore the 1930s was a very difficult time for them. Relief work was provided, but only for those who had made nothing at all during the season. Single men were employed to break stones in the Stokesby pit for 10s.0d. per four-day week. Married men received £1.

Caister skippers, however, were valued and were so prominent in the Yarmouth fleet, that in 1936, after the Home Fishing, a list, together with their boats, was published. There were 30 of them in a year when there were 110 Yarmouth registered steam drifters. The list included seven of the ten sons of old Mab Brown, Alf Mabby, Lew, Dick, George Raffy, Arthur Billy, Freddy Lightning, and Emmanuel Mangol, together with Ernie Crowe, Sid Cory, George Cockerill, Leonard and Albert Dawkins, Stephen Dyble, brothers Joe Roper, Leander Jay and John Shell George, Percy Rouse George, William Crip Green, Joe Gowen, Ben Titabee Haylett, Crabby Hudson, Arthur Liver Larner, senior and junior, Percy Minifer Nickerson, Reg Russell, Reg Symonds, Charlie Blunt Woodhouse, and Ted and George Woolston. These men were the lucky ones for it was said that another 40 Caister men with skipper's tickets were unable to get vessels and were working in lesser roles.

Eleven of these skippers worked for Bloomfields, which, in 1920, had been taken over by Mac Fisheries, becoming part of the Unilever Group, a merger which brought to the Ocean boats the names *Sunlight, Vim, Lifebouy* and *Lux*. The chairman of Unilever was called Cooper and in 1928 an award called the D'Arcy Cooper Challenge Cup was instituted to encourage the skippers in their work. From 1928 until 1938 it was awarded in two classes, steel drifters and wooden drifters and the presentations were made by Mrs. Cooper at Hill's restaurant, in King Street, Yarmouth. It was not awarded between 1939 and 1947, but in 1948 it was reinstated as the Lady Cooper Cup, but with only one class. It was last awarded in 1962, shortly before the Bloomfields fleet was sold.

The honours board for these awards is now in the Time and Tide Museum at Yarmouth. It shows several Caister winning skippers, together with their photographs. Jay George won the wooden class in 1930 as did his brother Roper in 1932 and 1935. Sid Cory won this class in 1934 and Ernie Crowe in 1936. Of the steel class Dick Brown won it in 1933 and Len Dawkins in 1936, 1937 and

88. Leander 'Jay' George, winner of the D'Arcy Cooper Cup in 1930.

89. Joe 'Roper' George, winner of the D'Arcy Cooper Cup in 1932 and 1935.

90. The steam drifter *Ut Prosim*, YH 169, skippered by Freddy 'Lightning' Brown, for Jack George of Yarmouth in the 1930s. She is seen entering Yarmouth harbour.

1938.

Freddy Lightning Brown was considered to be one of the 'luckiest' skippers in the Yarmouth fishing fleet, a term which meant very successful. He was the youngest of the ten brothers already mentioned, seven of who were drifter skippers. The family were late arrivals in the village, moving from California in 1912, when the terraced cottage they were living in was about to fall over the cliff.

Born in 1904, he started his fishing career at the age of 15, as a boy cook in the *Fortunatus*, a steam and sailing boat two years older than himself. Her wheelhouse was behind the pencil funnel and when possible she would sail to save coal. His brother Mabby was her skipper and that was how he got the berth. She fished the Spring and Summer voyages in 1919, but at the end of 20 weeks he came home with nothing. He could have had 10s a week sent home, but his mother had advised him to wait till the end, but the voyages were so poor that, being a share fisherman, there was nothing to show for his efforts.

Further voyages followed with the link to a Caister skipper being the key to getting the berth, first in the *Cheerio Lads*, skippered by his brother-in-law, Liver Larner, and then the *Helpmate* with Caister man Ben Green at the helm. Gaining his mates ticket he went in the *Oswy* with his brother Lew.

In 1927, at the age of 23, he got his skipper's ticket and, because his brothers were already successful skippers he was offered three boats, at a time when most new skippers were not getting any offers at all. Not sure what to do he asked his brothers for advice and was told to take the *Golden Sunbeam*, owned by Jack George of Yarmouth, as it was the most modern of the boats. He stayed with her for three years and did so well that Jack George offered him the pick of his fleet. Freddy chose the newest, the *Ut Prosim*, which he skippered until the outbreak of the war.

According to Freddy being a lucky skipper was more to do with good management and thoughtfulness than luck. As a new skipper he started with old gear, but did well enough to move on to boats with better gear, an important requirement for success, for it was wisely said that nets caught fish not boats. Freddy once did a voyage for Jack Plummer in the *Paradox II* to the 'Westards', as fishing from the West Country ports was termed. With him was Powley Dick Green of Winterton in the *Broadland*, a newer boat with old nets. The *Paradox II*, with new nets did much better. Old nets became misshapen in the water enabling the fish to slip through the mesh or fall out when the nets were hauled. New nets were essential in bad weather, but they were not popular with the men, as they had to be tanned on board, while the boat was in harbour.

Another part of being 'lucky' was to sign a good crew. The skipper would approach the best men, men known to work hard. Good skippers found it easy to recruit good crewman. Freddy always preferred those from the village, men he had known since childhood, as he considered those from Yarmouth to be less reliable.

As for thoughtfulness, if Freddy saw a lot of boats going in one direction he would go in the other. If the fishing was good one night, next day all the boats would return to that place, often drawing a blank, for in Freddy's opinion, once a shoal was heavily fished it would scatter. Again he would go elsewhere.

Being 'lucky' depended on a number of things, getting a good start would get a new skipper a good boat, good gear and a good crew. Add to this good instinct and you had Freddy Brown, 'lucky' skipper.

Fishing from the beach remained relatively steady during the inter-war years, with around eight to ten boats working at any one time. There was, a gradual renewal of the fleet, with motor boats being introduced, such as the *Emily Ethel*, owned by Emily Green, Wildawn's widow, the *Lily Georgina*, owned by Sprat Haylett's son George, and the *Endeavour* built locally for Skipper Woodhouse. It is at this point that Skipper, one of Caister's best-known characters, enters the story.

Skipper was born in the village in 1912 and was to spend his whole working life there. Most

91. Beach boats at Caister 1935, shortly after the Beach Company watch-house had been demolished. YH 77 is the *Rainbow* owned by Barney Barnard and YH 256 the *Lily Maud*, owned by Nat Brown.

92. Skipper Woodhouse's 'longshore boat *Seabird,* YH 271, on Caister Beach the day she arrived in 1960.

Caister seafaring boys leaving school in 1926 would have sought a berth as a boy cook on a steam drifter, but the fishing was not doing well and Skipper had always felt a living could be made fishing from the beach, so this is what he decided to do.

He started by 'pushing' a hand net for shrimps, which he would boil in his mother's washhouse copper, for customers of whom there was never a shortage. He also sold the herring and mackerel caught by the 'longshoremen round the village from a barrow, earning commission on the sales. In the summer he worked the deck chairs for Mab Brown. By 1929 he had saved enough money to buy a former ship's boat, from the steam drifter *Dashing Spray,* the name he gave her.

There was a saying, 'You can live orf 'longshorin if you eat and drink northin', but Skipper felt he would succeed if he made his own gear and so he persuaded the old men to teach him how to do so and how to use it. With this knowledge he embarked on the twin careers of 'longshore fishing and summer tripping.

In his first year he did very little fishing himself, spending his time taking out anglers to pursue their interest, but then he fitted his boat with sails taken from his father's old boat, the *Seek and Find* and with some herring nets, also garnered from his father, he set to work.

By 1934 Skipper had made enough money to buy a second craft, the motor boat *Endeavour,* and with this he revived the tripping business, taking parties out as far as the Cockle Lightship.

Over the years he turned his hand to every type of inshore fishing. In January, and in summer and autumn, he would 'do a bit of herrin', in the Roads, never much more that a mile out, using a dozen or so lints with a light on the dann buoy. He used to sell the catch around the village. In the spring he would drift for mackerel.

Shrimping he carried out all the year round with the catch still being boiled at home. In 1932 he started longlining for roker, using 800 to 1000 hooks. Also in the 1930s he went seine netting for sea trout, selling the catch to the Manor House Hotel. In this way Skipper succeeded in making a living from off the beach. He was also a member of the Beach Company.

With the beach culture being such a strong feature of the Caister tradition the Beach Company survived the disruption of the First World War, but the last mention of the use of a yawl (*Eclat*) was when she was working in conjunction with the lifeboat *Nancy Lucy* to stand by the Buckie steam drifter *Emily Reach* on the 28th/29th November 1919. The boat money entry for 5th March 1920 reads "*Emily Reaich*" Yawl & L.B. £15.17s.11d. She was never launched again on Company business, as the older men would no longer put to sea for speculative seeking voyages. The last entry of any description in the accounts for Company boats is for the 30th June 1926, when £14.17s.0d. was paid for painting the yawl and gig. In 1927 the *Eclat* was taken away to become the riverboat *Caister Maid* and in 1930 the gig *Ubique* was sold to be broken up for fencing timbers, after being damaged beyond repair during a launch.

Total reliance was then placed on the lifeboats to carry out the beachmen's lifesaving and salvage work. At the end of the war the large lifeboat was the third *Covent Garden* and the surf boat, the *Nancy Lucy*. Sprat Haylett was the coxswain, but he too was soon to suffer the fate of his Haylett cousins.

On the 29th January 1919 a lifeboat, with Sprat at the helm, was launched in a snowstorm to the steamer *Nimrod*, wrecked on the Barber. During this difficult service Sprat sustained serious internal injuries and having taken to his bed complications set in. On the 15th March he died at the age of 54. He had been going off in the lifeboat since 1883 and had been on 158 services, from which 805 lives had been saved, 310 of them when he was coxswain. At his funeral one reporter described the Caister Cemetery as, 'Thickly studded with graves of lifeboatmen who have sacrificed

93. Boats on Caister beach c1925. The boat with crossed masts is the yawl *Eclat*. Behind her is the gig *Ubique*. The lifeboat is the *Nancy Lucy*. In the background can be seen the Beach Company watch-house, the coastguard lookout and the Manor House hotel.

94. The Caister lifeboat *Charles Burton*, 1940. She was the last pulling and sailing lifeboat to be stationed at Caister. Her replacement by a motor lifeboat in 1941 spelt the end for the Beach Company.

their lives in heroic efforts to save lives of others, Caister Cemetery will ever be a revered place of pilgrimage. Now another of the "bravest of the brave" rejoins old comrades who had gone before him and still more memories will cluster round the spot'.[74]

Charlie Lacock became the new coxswain and one of the first matters he had to attend to was the replacement of the *Covent Garden*. On the 12th March 1919 she was launched to the schooner *Intrepide*, aground on the Middle Scroby. This would prove to be her last service for when in September she was inspected it was found that her dropped keel was not working properly, so the R.N.L.I.'s Reserve No. 1 lifeboat was sent to the station. In the event the repairs to the *Covent Garden* were thought to be too costly, so the Reserve boat, ex *James Leath*, became permanent under her former name.

The two lifeboats, *Nancy Lucy* and *James Leath* remained at Caister until the end of the 1920s, but were rarely launched, the impact of the improvement to vessels being now fully felt. Elsewhere the R.N.L.I. was deploying motor lifeboats and such boats were placed at Cromer in 1923 and at Gorleston in 1924.

The question of closing one of the two Caister stations had been raised as early as 1914, and once these local motor lifeboats were in place this became a reality. The No.2 Station was closed in November 1929, and the *Nancy Lucy* was sold for conversion into a houseboat. The *James Leath* was also removed at this time and the now single station received a new boat, the *Charles Burton*.

The *Charles Burton* was transferred from Grimsby. She was an old boat, built in 1904. The R.N.L.I. had stopped building pulling and sailing lifeboats, but had yet to develop a motorboat suitable for beach launching. The *Charles Burton's* first service was not until the 16th August 1930 when she was launched to the French steam trawler *Jean Dore*, stranded on the Middle Caister Shoal. She stood by as the rising tide floated the trawler off.

She continued to serve until the early years of the Second World War, but whereas in days gone by the lifeboat was launched to schooners, barques and brigantines, the *Charles Burton's* casualties were steam drifters, steam trawlers and small sailing boats, which in 1937 included Caister's own *Sea Bird*. By then Skipper's father, Joe, had taken over from Charlie Lacock, as coxswain.

The dramatic fall in salvage work, both in terms of quantity, and quality, was one of the reasons why the Beach Company suffered a major blow at this time, the demolition of its watch-house. For most of its working life the fortunes of the Company were closely tied to the Clowes family. Thomas Clowes became Lord of the Manors of Caister in 1803, which included ownership of the beach. It is probably then that he gave permission for the Company to erect a watch-house and lookout, receiving a share of all salvage money by way of rent. Surprisingly there is no documentation to this effect, but the arrangement is highlighted in later Manor sale particulars.[75]

In 1857 Thomas was succeeded by his son John who continued the arrangement. He was a good friend of the beachmen, recognised by the fact that they displayed his portrait in an honoured place by the door of the watch-house.

On his death in 1877 the lordship passed to his widow, Maria Dorothy, and it was with her that the Clowes links with Caister began to slacken. In the early 1870s John was involved in the development of Norfolk Square, the first building project to take place on Yarmouth's North Drive. He built the first three houses on the north side and it was to one of these that his widow moved.

In 1894 she sold the Manor House to the Caister & Sheringham Hotel & Land Company, which built a large extension on the seaward side to create the Manor House hotel.[76] Throughout this period her son, Frank, was the steward of the Manors and maintained the involvement with the beachmen, as secretary of the local lifeboat committee.

Maria died in 1918 and that year the Manors were sold to Anthony Traynier of Yarmouth, a man who had no affinity with the beachmen nor their calling. Neither was he impressed with the value of the salvage share by way of rent, which in 1924 averaged a paltry £10 per annum. Wishing to maximise the income from his beach rights he first sought payment for the tents and huts the beachmen ran during the holiday season. They refused to pay, winning their point in the local court, but Traynier took them to the High Court and managed to get the verdict overturned.

In 1924 Traynier moved to London, but later when he returned to live in Gorleston, he decided to give the beachmen notice to quit the watch-house. Allowed six months from the 27th September 1934 to deliver up possession of the 'lookout and shed' the beachmen initially refused and were once more taken to court but, realising they could not win, they settled. Traynier immediately demolished the building and even sold the very sand hill on which it had stood to a local builder.

Left without a home the beachmen approached the R.N.L.I. who reluctantly let them relocate to the lifeboat store shed, bringing their old call-out bell with them. On the 15th January 1936, at a meeting of the Company held in the lifeboat shed, the 22 members present elected a committee of five to review the rules. The committee reported on the 22nd January and the revised rules were duly approved. They were a very simplified version of the originals, reflecting the now infrequent nature of the salvage work.

The inter-war years also witnessed the closure of the coastguard station. In 1918 the coastguard consisted of a Chief Officer and five men, but in 1923 the establishment was reduced to one senior coastguard and one other man. It was closed altogether in 1933.

After the war onshore lifesaving at Caister was still in the hands of the Rocket Company, which came under the control of the Board of Trade in 1923, but still supervised by the coastguards. It had been manned by volunteers since the latter part of the 19th century, men who were not seaman

95. The Caister Rocket Company, March 1933.

Back row, left to right; A. Thomson, F. Humphrey, E. Julier, R. Bessey, A. Myhill, R. Trett, B. Nickerson, T. Smith, A. Dyball. Front row; R Brown, C. Larkman, R. Chapman, J. Julier, Lieut. J. Maguire M.B.E. RN, T. Rowe (Coastguard Station officer), T. Jones, T. Humphrey, W. Horth, H Bird.

so they would be readily available.

In March 1931 the Rocket Company assembled to carry out its quarterly exercises in a heavy snowstorm. This attracted the attention of a Yarmouth Mercury reporter who wrote, ' At the order "action" the company set about their various duties and transported their life-saving apparatus to an adjacent field at a point immediately opposite an assumed wreck. A rocket with two hundred fathoms of thin rope attached was fired and sent roaring seawards by Mr. Joe Julier. The wreck party secured the line and communication being established the breeches buoy was speedily sent out by means of the whip and a rescue smartly effected'.[77]

The members then took part in a 'heaving the cane' competition, which was won by Reg Trett. The cane had a line attached at one end and a pound of lead at the other. Tom Humphrey, the blacksmith, who had held the record with a heave of 37 yards, was on that occasion wide of the mark.

The reporter also recorded that, 'The rescue of the crew of sixteen from the Varna, which ran ashore in January 1897, was the smartest piece of work any of the present crew can recall, and another praiseworthy rescue was that of six men from the steamsloop Gertrude of Bremen, in 1902, when that coal laden vessel ran ashore near Dinah's Gap in a terrible storm. A more recent feat was the rescue… of the crew of seven from the Moorside, in 1919. On this occasion the struggle along the cliffs was effected at night in most treacherous weather, and although communication was speedily effected by the rocket line, the shipwrecked crew did not venture into the breeches buoy until daylight.' The rocket company was also disbanded in 1933.

6. 1939 TO THE PRESENT DAY

As far as Great Britain was concerned the Second World War officially started on the 3rd September 1939. For Caister this meant a repeat of the events of 25 years earlier, when the naval reservists were called up and the village owned drifters were requisitioned for war service.

As luck would have it, the central depot for the Royal Naval Patrol Service, in which many of the RNR men served, was established a few miles down the coast at the Sparrow's Nest in Lowestoft. It was the nearest British establishment to Nazi occupied Europe.

The Caister men who had opted for the Patrol Service reported to the Nest. From there they were posted to the various requisitioned and purpose built trawlers, drifters, and other small craft, to carry out minesweeping, submarine chasing, and harbour work in home waters and around the world.

Being an RNR Skipper Freddy Brown was given command of the Hull trawler *Istria* and sent to patrol the entrances to Scapa Flow, after the *Royal Oak* had been sunk there by the German submarine U-47. He was then deployed escorting the Trinity House vessel *Northern Isles* around Scotland, because her master and crew would not go out unaccompanied, having seen so many submarines. While on this duty he was convinced he had sunk a U-boat. He fired a pattern of depth charges and saw a submarine surface, then quickly disappear again, but he could not convince the authorities that he had made 'a kill', as there had to be evidence of wreckage or, as Freddy put it, you had to have the 'gift of the gab'. To rub salt into the wound he was carpetted for damaging his vessel. Apparently it was too slow for the work and was unable to clear the pattern of depth charges quickly enough. The explosion wrecked the *Istria's* dynamo and Freddy had to take her

96. 'Skipper' John Woodhouse 1912-1999. The last of the Beachmen.

97. George 'Raffy' Brown, Chief-skipper in charge of the RN drifter *Fisher Boy.* He received the M.B.E., for exemplary war service.

into port for repairs. When he got there he took himself off to bed, but was quickly hauled out to go through the red tape. Freddy recalled that skippers found it hard to adjust to the Royal Navy bull, whereas the Navy men considered the skippers to be rough diamonds who were not prepared to accept naval discipline.

With the *Istria* in port Freddy returned to the Nest for a posting. After a short stint on the Thames he was sent to Malta, in an island class minesweeper, with the rank of Skipper/Lieutenant, and two skippers under his command. This boat was a purpose built sub-chaser, which worked as part of a fleet led by a Commander. He spent the rest of the war there.

All Freddy's brothers were in the Patrol Service. Richard was at Harwich on examination duty; Samuel, Ernest and Alf Mabby did similar work on the Clyde, but not in uniform, as tended to be the case with the older men. George Raffy was a Chief-skipper in charge of the Lowestoft drifter *Fisher Boy*, which was attached to *H.M.S. Vernon*. She and four other drifters were fitted out to recover mines by trawling and together were known as Vernon's private navy. They carried out this task throughout the war, but in June 1940, when the evacuation from Dunkirk began, the flotilla was sent to assist. Raffy made seven trips, rescuing nearly 1,400 soldiers, while under fire. Later, in January 1941, when on examination duty at Brightlingsea, *Fisher Boy* was attacked by a German plane, an M.E.110, which dropped bombs and straffed her with machine gun fire. The drifter crew returned fire with their Lewis guns and brought the plane down. For his courage and devotion to duty Raffy was awarded the M.B.E (Military Division).

Not all those called up were as fortunate, for once the conflict was over another 40 names were added to the village war memorial.

98. 'The Brown Boys', the ten sons of Emmanuel 'Mab' Brown.
Back row; left to right; Freddy 'Lightning', Samuel 'Jidd', Ernest 'White Nob'. Alf 'Mabby', George 'Raffy', Arthur 'Billy'. Front row; Dick, Emmanuel 'Mangol', Lew, Henry 'Henduck'.

99. The steam drifter *Animation,* YH 138, c1930. Built in Lowestoft in 1925 she was owned by Fred Haylett, Ernest Haylett and George Woolston until Woolston became sole owner in 1936. She was one of the five Caister owned drifters to be returned after service in the Second World War.

Fearing invasion, the order was given for potential landing beaches to be defended. Once mined and festooned with barbed wire Caister beach was placed out of bounds. Tank traps and pillboxes were also constructed. Despite these restrictions Skipper Woodhouse continued to fish from the beach, taking care to avoid the mines, even advising others of their whereabouts, and getting those in front of the lifeboat shed moved It was while he was working in this way that he was mistaken for a German by a German. In 1942 an enemy plane ditched off the coast. One of the crew managed to swim ashore, but got caught up in the barbed wire on the beach. Looking out to sea he saw Skipper and his crew in their boat. Thinking this was the rest of his crew, in their rubber dinghy, he began to shout and wave, in the process alerting the local Home Guard to his whereabouts. The rest of the aircrew were picked up at Hemsby.

Although unnamed, in 1941 Caister had the honour of being selected by the Illustrated Magazine to represent all the villages vulnerable to invasion. A photographer covered the preparations being made for a possible invasion, accompanied by the American film star, Ann Dvorak. The piece was entitled 'Invasion Village'.

With the war over the serving fishermen were de-mobbed and the requisitioned drifters were returned to their owners. During the black days before the war many men had forsaken the life of a fisherman and there were now fewer willing to resume the unpredictable work, although sufficient remained to witness the demise of the once great herring fishery.

The *Rose* was broken up in 1940, but six other Caister owned drifters returned to port namely, the *A Rose*, *Achievable*, *Animate*, *Animation*, *George Albert* and *Speranza*. Jack Plummer never fished the *Speranza* after the war and in 1951 he sold her to be broken up, having bought the *Rosebay*. Prior to this he had netted one or two boats, belonging to other owners, from his pre-war stock of nets. He fished the *Rosebay* until January 1956, when, having slipped a disc and seeing that the writing was on the wall for the industry, he sold her and retired from boat owning. His connection with the sea continued, for that year he became coxswain of the lifeboat.

George Woolston sold the *Animation* to George Newson in 1945. The following year Crabby Hudson sold the *A Rose* to a Norwegian owner, who wanted to use her for trading. In November 1948 he died leaving his other boat, *Achievable*, to his widow Laura. Netted by others, Laura ran the boat for a number of years, before selling her to be broken up.

Tready Haylett sold the *Animate* to his son Gordon Goee, in 1947. Goee fished her until the Home Fishing of 1957, then following the fate of the others, she too was sold to be broken up. In 1950 George Haylett sold the *George Albert* to be converted into a Sea Scout training ship, her engine and boilers having been removed. By then he was part owner of the *Ocean Guide*, which, he and two partners had bought from Bloomfields in 1946. In 1954 he bought the *Ocean Rambler*, but the following year both vessels went to the breakers yard.

Immediately after the war it was not obvious that the herring fishery was in its death throes, especially to three new Caister consortia who ventured forth with the *Craiglea, Ekede* and *Scadaun*. The *Craiglea* was an old boat, which in 1948 Charles Eastick sold to Edward Beazer of Yarmouth and Percy Hayhoe of Caister, but some four years later they had had enough and sold her back to Eastick.

The other two boats were somewhat different. These were built towards the end of the war as motor fishing boats (MFBs) for the Patrol Service. After the war the Government wanted to encourage the revival of the fishing industry and so a scheme was set up whereby they were prepared to sell these boats to ex servicemen, with the aid of a start up loan. As an additional

100. The motor fishing boat *Ekede,* YH 175, c1950. Built in 1946 for the Patrol Service she was bought in 1947 by five Caister skippers. The venture was not a success and she was sold in 1958.

101. Alf 'Mabby' Brown and the crew of the *Wydale,* YH 105, Prunier Trophy winners in 1950.

incentive these new owners would be entitled to £5,000, should they survive in business for five years. This was an attractive offer for men who had never owned before.

The *Ekede* was bought in 1947 by five men, Henry Barnard, Arthur Liver Larner, Raffy Brown and his brother Freddy, together with their nephew Lew Brown. The boat's name was created from the initials of their wives forenames. Having acquired the boat they did not have enough capital to buy the gear so they approached Jack Plummer who agreed to net her on a fifty-fifty basis, which he thought generous, reiterating the old saying, 'nets catch fish not boats'. Jack's beatsters were also employed to mend the nets.

In the event the venture was not a success. Both Freddy Brown and Jack Plummer put this down to the fact that all the owners were experienced skippers and thus it was difficult for one of them to run the voyage without interference from the others. It was a case of too many cooks spoiling the broth. Jack was also of the opinion that now they were owners, they did not think they had to work so hard.

In 1948 they mortgaged the boat to the Herring Industry Board, but in May 1949, Freddy paid off his part of the mortgage and sold his share in the boat to the others, preferring instead to skipper the *Achievable*, owned by Mrs. Hudson and netted by Jack Plummer. The other four owners carried on until early 1958, when having paid off the mortgage, they sold the boat to Frank Instone of London.

Paul Barnard and Clifford Shreeve bought the *Scadaun* in 1948. They too secured a mortgage from the Herring Industry Board and tried to make a go of it, but in 1956 they discharged the mortgage and sold her to a consortium of Scottish owners.

It was during this post war period that Alf Mabby Brown became the only Caister man to win the coveted Prunier Trophy, being one of only three Yarmouth skippers to do so, the others both hailing from Winterton.

The Prunier Trophy was the idea of restaurateur Madame Prunier, who wanted to promote the herring as a food. It was awarded to the boat landing the biggest catch of fresh herring in one shot either at Yarmouth or Lowestoft, during a set period. First awarded in 1936 it lapsed during the war years and Mabby won it in 1950, in the Eastick owned drifter *Wydale*.

On the 23rd October that year she came into port with a shot of 250¼ crans. Mabby had cast his nets 8 miles N.E. of the Smith's Knoll buoy. Her total catch amounted to over 300 cran, but some of the nets, with about 60 crans, had been handed over to the *Harry Eastick*. Hauling had begun about 10pm and was not completed until 11 o'clock the next morning. In 1961 the *Wydale* had the distinction of being the last steam drifter to fish from the United Kingdom, when working out of Shields.

The last Caister owned drifter to fish out of Yarmouth was the *Rosebay*. In 1956 Goee Haylett borrowed money from his mother and Norford Suffling to buy the boat from Jack Plummer. Freddy Brown moved with her as skipper, but he eventually gave up, as he did not feel the boat was being sufficiently well maintained. A patch had been welded to a plate, but it was not checked and it let in water. It had to be repaired during a voyage and thus valuable fishing time was lost. The boat was fished until the Home Fishing of 1960. Early in 1961 she was sold to a Dutch Company to be broken up, thus ending the long tradition of Caister deep-sea boat owning. Five years later the last Prunier Trophy was awarded and the once great Yarmouth herring fishery was no more.

The Beach Company fared no better. Now that the beachmen were totally reliant on the R.N.L.I.

102. The steam drifter *Rosebay*, YH 78. Heading for the Gut at North Shields, 1955.
Left to right; John 'Jumbo' Amis, ——, ——, Freddy Brown (in the wheelhouse), Billy Read, Benny Read, Bertie Brown. She was the last Caister owned deep-sea fishing boat.

103. Caister Lifeboat *Jose Neville* in Yarmouth Harbour after the service to the Lowestoft trawler *Kirkley,* April 1963. She was the last R.N.L.I lifeboat at Caister.

Left to right, Benny Read, Alf 'Mabby' Brown, George Codman, rescued man, Harry Pascoe, rescued man, rescued man, rescued man, Jack Plummer, David Woodhouse, rescued man.

for both boat and watch-house its inspectors began to put pressure on to wind the Company up, because they did not like money being paid to people who had not gone off in the boat.

The Company rule changes of 1936 had done away with sick pay, but had retained the right of a widow to put a man in to work her late husband's share. As a compromise the beachmen agreed to disband the Company once they had the benefit of a motor lifeboat. The R.N.L.I.'s hand was strengthened further with the onset of the Second World War. Many of the Caister beachmen were called up and the lifeboat had to be manned by men from outside the Company. This had the effect of destabilising the Company payment system.

There had been talk of placing a motor lifeboat at Caister since 1938, but it was not until May 1941 that the *Jose Neville* arrived on station, thereby bringing the curtain down on the Beach Company, a Caister seafaring institution that had been active for 150 years. It had the distinction of being the last village company to close its books.

The *Jose Neville* was a Liverpool type motorboat, paid for from a legacy given by Mrs. Ellen Neville. She was a different proposition to what the beachmen had been used to. Being carriage launched by tractor, there was no longer the need for large numbers of 'larnchers' and for the first time a motor mechanic was necessary to maintain the engine of the lifeboat and the tractor. As Skipper Woodhouse was familiar with motorboat engines he got the job. The new operational arrangements meant that a replacement shed was required, one in which the lifeboat could be kept. This was built of corrugated asbestos and today houses the Lifeboat Visitor Centre.

While on station the *Jose Neville* performed a number of services, her last being the most memorable. Just after midnight on the 13th December 1963 a mayday signal was sent from a vessel close to the North-West Scroby buoy. She proved to be the trawler *Loch Lorgan*. The lifeboat was launched and on reaching the casualty it was found she was aground in a breaking sea, with an alarming list to starboard. Taking a calculated risk coxswain Jack Plummer ran the lifeboat along her port side and, after securing her with lines, the seven men on board jumped to safety. For this outstanding piece of seamanship Jack Plummer was awarded the R.N.L.I.'s Bronze Medal. He was later awarded the B.E.M.

In 1964 the *Jose Neville* was replaced by the *Royal Thames*, a lifeboat destined to be the last R.N.L.I. boat at Caister. During the mid-1960s the Institution revised its operational practices and after the fast lifeboat *Khami* was placed at Gorleston, in 1967, it was decided that she would cover the Caister area of operations. As a result in October 1969 the *Royal Thames* was taken away and the station closed. During its days as an R.N.L.I. station the Caister lifeboats had been responsible for saving 1,814 lives, more than any other station at that time.

The retiring coxswain, Jack Plummer, saw the closure as disappointing but inevitable, but not all in the village were prepared to accept that Caister's fine tradition of lifesaving was now a matter for the history books. A public meeting was called and out of this came the Caister Volunteer Rescue Service (C.V.R.S).

Skipper Woodhouse was one of the leading lights and it was him who provided a 16-foot fibreglass boat, with an engine, to give continuity while funds were being raised for a new lifeboat. In 1970 this boat was joined by an inflatable with an engine, bought with money raised by the children of the Caister Secondary Modern School.

These boats served the station well, until 1973 when the C.V.R.S bought the ex R.N.L.I. lifeboat *Viking*, which was similar in many respects to the first motor lifeboat at Caister, the *Jose Neville*. The opportunity was given for her to be named by whoever gave the largest donation. This proved to be B.P. Development. The wife of the local manager was invited to perform the naming

104. Coxswain Benny Read with the author's son James aboard the C.V.R.S lifeboat *Shirley Jean Adye,* 1986.

105. The lifeboat *Bernard Matthews* being tractor launched while the crew of the inshore lifeboat *Jim Davidson* look on.

ceremony. It was not until the covers were removed that she saw that the boat had been named after her, the *Shirley Jean Adye*. Alf Mabby Brown, son of the Prunier Trophy winner, became her first coxswain and in 1981 the popular Benny Read succeeded him.

During her stay at the station the *Shirley Jean Adye* made close on 70 services, rescuing nearly 60 people. The vessels assisted were largely small motorboats, but in the 1980s she started to be called out to rig supply vessels, as the oil/gas industry became well established. By then she was beginning to show her age and despite an extensive refit, it was decided that an appeal should be launched to raise money for a new boat. It was then that the idea of a locally run volunteer lifeboat, to carry on the tradition of the men who 'Never Turn Back', really caught the public imagination and it has never looked back since.

The appeal was launched on the 23rd April 1987 by the Mayor of Yarmouth and Michelle Newman from BBC 'Look East'. The target was an ambitious £400,000. In many respects Skipper Woodhouse was the face of the appeal, appearing twice on the Wogan show and in 1991 being the subject of a 'This is Your Life' programme. In 1993 he received the M.B.E. for his efforts,

Entertainers Russ Abbott and Bobby Davro supported a charity event in 1987 and H.R.H. Prince Charles endorsed the appeal when in 1988 he visited the station and was given a trip in the *Shirley Jean Adye* by Benny Read and the crew. He was to visit again in 1995.

In 1990 comedian Jim Davidson organised a number of end of the pier shows at Yarmouth, the proceeds from which were used to purchase a new inshore boat that bore his name. Eventually sufficient funds had been raised to order a replacement for the *Shirley Jean Adye*, which arrived at Caister on the 15th May 1991. She was named the *Bernard Matthews* in acknowledgment of the generous support given by the Norfolk Turkey farmer.

Sadly on the 1st September that same year coxswain Benny Read was tragically killed when the

106. 'Boxing the Catch', Caister 7th April 2010. The 'longshore boat *Shetland Sun*, YH 394 had been fishing off Winterton and returned with a catch of sprats, pilchards and herring. Her crew is seen shaking sprats from the net. Left to right; Jack Waitt, Aaron 'Bubba' Thurlow, Jason 'Dodge' Miller, the boat's owner.

maroons he was setting off exploded in his chest. Caister mourned another lifesaving hero. Dick Thurlow replaced him as coxswain and both lifeboats performed valuable services until they in turn were replaced, the one by the *Jim Davidson OBE*, in 2002 and the other by the *Bernard Matthews II* in 2004, for which a new shed was built. At this juncture Dick Thurlow stood down as coxswain and Paul Williams took over.

Today the sea story continues. In 2009 the old lifeboat shed was converted into a Lifeboat Visitor Centre with, as its main attraction, the *Shirley Jean Adye*, albeit in R.N.L.I. livery rather than the distinctive orange she wore when on service with the C.V.R.S. A pool of 18 men is available to provide crews for the lifeboats. None bear the surnames Haylett, George, Brown, Hodds or Read, but several have another link with Caister's seafaring past and that is that they run their own 'longshore fishing boats.

There is an active 'longshore fishery at Caister, although none of the fishermen are able to work at it full time, most having other jobs or being retired. There are 10-12 boats, which in the main stand together behind the dunes, just along from the lifeboat shed. Those who wish to sell their catches are licensed and are subject to quotas set by the Marine and Fisheries Agency. Traditional methods are used to catch the fish, drift netting for herring, sprats and pilchards, long lining for cod.

This small fishery and the volunteer lifeboats provide a picturesque and active link with the village's seafaring past, a working tribute to the men who Never Turn Back.

Notes and References

1   The first Act for this purpose was given the Royal Assent in 1711 (10 ANNE, 1). The work was completed under a revival of that Act in 1723 (10 GE0I,8).

2   Sandred, Karl Inge, The Place-Names of Norfolk, English Place-Name Society, 1996, p3.

3   Ekwall, Eilert, The Concise Oxford Dictionary of English Place-Names, London, 1936, Fourth Edition 1974, p81.

4   For the Roman period see, Darling, Margaret, and Gurney, David, Caister-on-Sea, Excavations by Charles Green 1951-1955, East Anglian Archaeology, 60, 1993; and Gurney, David, Outposts of the Roman Empire, Norfolk Archaeological Trust, 2002.

5   The name was found on a small-inscribed bronze sheet in 1986.

6   Clarke, R. Rainbird, East Anglia. Thames and Hudson, 1960, p149.

7   EAA 60, p255. Fursa's monastery is usually thought to have been within the walls of Burgh Castle.

8   Ekwall, p79.

9   For Grimulf the Dane see, West, J.R. ed., St Benet of Holme 1020-1210. Norfolk Record Society, 2, 1932 pp3 and 33. For Thurketel Heyng see, Sawyer, P.H., Anglo Saxon Charters, London, 1968, p428.

10 Domesday Book, Norfolk, Phillimore, 1984.

11 Cornford, Barbara, Medieval Flegg, The Larks Press, 2002.

12 Caister formerly comprised two ecclesiastical parishes, East and West. These were combined in 1608. In 1926 the then civil parish of Caister was divided into East and West. Most of the activity described in this book took place in East Caister. Caister Castle is in West Caister.

13 A full account of this dispute is given in Henry Swinden's, The History and Antiquities of the Ancient Burgh of Great Yarmouth, Ch X11, Norwich, 1772. Comments by Henry Manship and further information from Charles John Palmer are given in the latter's, The History of Great Yarmouth by Henry Manship, and its Continuation, Meall, 1854.

14 Swinden p364.

15 Swinden p356. This seems to be the ship referred to as the *Admiral de Sluys* in Palmer's Manship p172.

16 Swinden p358.

17 Swinden p362.

18 Swinden p362/3.

19 This ditch can still be seen between White Gate farm and the Catholic cemetery, on the Yarmouth Road.

20 Palmer's Manship Vol.1, p173.

21 State Papers Westminster 8th November 1565.

22 Muster of Seamen, 21st December 1664, Raynham Hall.

23 Swinden p196.

24 Records of the Corporation of the Trinity House. Historical Manuscripts Commission, Appendix to the 8th Report.

25 The story of the Beach Companies is told in the author's book The Beachmen.

26 The records of the Great Yarmouth Admiralty Court are to be found in the Norfolk Record Office (NRO), reference C/16.

27 The owners of the *Betsey* appealed the local decision in the High Court of Delegates. in London. The relevant papers are in the National Archives (NA), reference DEL 7/2 Fol. 234-244.

28 NA, ADM 7/386, Registers of Protection from Impressment.

29 NA. Sea Fencible Pay Lists. ADM 28/17-20.

30 NA. Customs Outport Books, Great Yarmouth CUST 97/33.

31 NA, CUST 97/33.

32 NA, CUST 97/33.

33 NRO, C/Sca 2/63.

34 NRO, C/Sce 1/9 pp55-56.

35 History, Gazetteer, and Directory of Norfolk, 1836, p306.

36 Rules and Regulations of the Caister Company of Beachmen. 1848.

37 The current whereabouts of the Beach Company account books, 1842-78, 1885-1939, is unknown. Microfilm copies of the five books are in the N.R.O.

38 Norwich Mercury (NM) 19th April 1856.

39 NRO, C/16/7.

40 NM 23rd March 1833.

41 NM 28th February 1835.

42 Manby, Capt. G. W., Practical Observations on the Preservation of Mariners from Stranded Vessels and the Prevention of Shipwreck, 1827.

43 Northumberland Report on lifeboats, 1851.

44 There is a possibility that the *Phoenix* survived because later in 1845 the Newport Company was operating a boat of that name, which had been built

in the same year as the lost yawl, 1843.

45 NC 8th February 1845.

46 The identity of the lifeboat coxswains before Philip George is far from certain. The sequence which best fits the available evidence is: Benjamin Hodds (Junior), 1845-1852 (died), Robert George Junior, 1852-1863 (died), Samuel 'Nobody' George, 1863-1865, Philip George, 1865-1887.

47 NC 18th December 1858.

48 NM 17th July 1847.

49 NM 7th August 1875.

50 NM 5th August 1876.

51 It has generally been thought that Tan Lane took its name from the tanning copper associated with a net warehouse at its seaward end. This warehouse, however, was not built until the early 1870s, whereas the name Tan Lane predates 1851.

52 Nall, John Greaves, Chapters on the East Anglian Coast, 1866, p421.

53 NA, BT98/831-839.

54 Skipper Woodhouse in conversation.

55 NM 20th February 1869.

56 NM 2nd January 1869.

57 Yarmouth Independent (YI) 6th February 1875.

58 YI 6th November 1875.

59 YI 6th November 1875.

60 YI 6th November 1875.

61 YI 4th December 1875.

62 YI 20th November 1875.

63 YI 28th July 1885.

64 Staniland, C.J., Lifeboats and Lifeboatmen, Part II Norfolk and Suffolk, English Illustrated Magazine, 1885/6. p397. Those lost were John Burton, Fred Haylett, Joe Haylett, George Hodds, James King, William Knowles, John Riches and John Sutton.

65 YM 16th November 1901.

66 YM 14th December 1901.

67 YM 23rd November 1901.

68 The Caister Life-Boat Disaster, The Lifeboat, 1st February 1902. p302.

69 Eastern Daily Press, July 1971.

70 Harris, G.H., Transactions of the Norfolk and Norwich Naturalists Society, (TN NNS), Annual Notes on the Herring Fishery of Yarmouth, 1899.

71 An account of these warehouses is given in, Green, Charles, Herring-Nets and Beasters. An Essay in Industrial Archaeology, Norfolk Archaeology Vol. XXXIV, Part IV, 1969.

72 Staniland, p399.

73 TNNNS 1928, p669.

74 YI 22nd March 1919.

75 In his letter to the Yarmouth Independent of the 6th November 1875, John Clowes stated that the Beach Company had been established about 70 years.

76 This hotel with its prominent mock timber-framed, extension, was constantly under threat from the sea, a fight which is finally lost in 1941. The Never Turn Back public house stands in its former grounds.

77 YM March 1931.

Select Bibliography

Bensley, Mick.   The Rescues of the Caister Lifeboats, BEN GUNN, 2008.

Cannell, John.   Home from the Sea, Caister Lifeboat Publishing, 1996.
The men who never turn back, Caister Lifeboat Publishing, 2000.
Norfolk Independence, 2007.

Hawkins, L.W.   The Prunier Herring Trophy, privately published, 1982.
The Ocean Fleet of Yarmouth, privately published, 1983.

Higgins, David.   The Beachmen, Terence Dalton, 1987.
The Winterton Story, Phoenix Publications, 2009.

Leach, Nicholas.   Never Turn Back, Tempus, 2001.

Malster, Robert.   Saved from the Sea. Terence Dalton, 1974.

Tooke, Colin.   Caister Beach Boats and Beachmen, Poppyland Publishing, 1986.
Skipper Jack, Poppyland Publishing, 1988.
Caister. 2000 Years a Village, Tookes Books, 2000.
The Great Yarmouth Herring Industry, Tempus, 2006.

Index of People

Illustrations in bold type

Index of Vessels

Mabel (brig)	48	Queen Alexandra YH 546 (sd)	57	Thalia YH 1066 (smack)	64,68
Maria (schooner)	45			The Brothers (shrimper)	53
Mark Lane (lifeboat)	55	Rainbow YH 77 (beach boat)	**85**	Thor II (ship)	**69**
Mary Ann (beach boat)	44	Ralph Hall Caine YH 447 (st)	80	Two Friends YH 607 (smack)	62,66
Masterpiece YH 360 (smack)	66	Ranger YH 296 (lugger)	44	Two Sisters (smack)	61,62
Mon Ami YH 178 (sd)	79,80	Red Jacket (yawl)	37,39,45,**73**		
Moorside (schooner)	**8**,90	Red Jacket (smack)	60	Ubique (gig)	**26**,87,**87**
Nancy Lucy (lifeboat)	58,59,87,**87**,88	Rescuer (lifeboat)	62,**62**	Ut Prosim YH 169 (sd)	84,**84**
Nell YH 868 (smack)	65	Resolution (HMS)	20		
Neptunus (ship)	30,**30**	Roburn (HMD)	76,**76**	Varna (ss)	90
Nile (ship)	**69**	Rose YH 971 (sd)	82,93	Venus (yawl)	21
Nimrod (ss)	87	Rosebay YH 78 (sd)	93,94,96,**96**	Venus YH 977 (smack)	66,**66**
Norford Suffling YH 45 (sd)	79,80	Rover (brig)	47	Vernon (HMS)	92
Northern Isles (Trinity vessel)	91	Royal Oak (HMS)	91	Victory (lugger)	43
Notus (gig)	37	Royal Sovereign (pleasure boat)	40	Vigilant YH 569 (smack)	62
Ocean Dawn YH 47 (sd)	81,**81**	Royal Thames (lifeboat)	98	Viking (lifeboat)	98
Ocean Guide YH 24 (sd)	94	Salamander YH 411 (sd)	67	Voltigeur (barque)	47
Ocean Lifebuoy YH 29 (sd)	83	Sanscrit YH 721 (sd)	79,80	Vrieheid (man of war)	13,**13**
Ocean Lux YH 84 (sd)	83	Saucy Jack (lugger)	28		
Ocean Rambler YH 725 (sd)	94	Scadaun YH 384 (mfb)	94,95	Waterloo (brig)	30
Ocean Retriever YH 307 (sd)	71,77,81,82	Sea Bird (beach boat)	**86**,89	Wave (schooner)	47
Ocean Retriever II YH 33 (sd)	81	Seamew (ss)	68	Welcome YH 635 (smack)	66
Ocean Sunlight YH 167 (sd)	83	Seamew YH 710 (smack)	63,66	Wild Wave (schooner)	50
Ocean Treasure YH 574 (sd)	71,**75**,77,81	Seek and Find YH 133 (beach boat)	86	William YH 832 (smack)	66
Ocean Vim YH 88 (sd)	83	Seven Brothers (lugger)	44	William and John YH 652 (smack)	62
Olivae YH 73 (sd)	79,80	Shade of Evening YH 229 (smack)	62,65,**65**	William and Mary (beach boat)	44
Oriental (ship)	49	Shamrock PH (sd)	58	Wydale YH 105 (sd)	**95**,96
Orion YH 112 (smack)	61	Shetland Sun YH 394 (beach boat)	**99**		
Osprey YH 476 (sd)	69	Shirley Jean Adye (lifeboat)	98,**98**,99,100	Young England (barque)	50
Oswy YH 34 (sd)	84	Silver Quest YH 658 (beach boat)	**9**	Young John	29
		Snowdrop YH 708 (sd)	57	Young Thomas (beach boat)	44
Paradox YH 951 (smack)	64,**64**	Solomon YH 784 (smack)	63,66		
Paradox II YH 710 (sd)	**68**,69,78,82,85	Soudan (ship)	54	Zephyr (yawl)	28,29,30,37,39,45,46
Pernicity (gig)	22	Sparkling Foam YH 493 (sd)	63,65	Zephyr II (yawl)	45,51,52,53,**53**,65,**65**,68
Phoenix (yawl)	35,101	Speranza YH 382 (smack)	**63**,64,69	Zephyr YH 494 (smack)	61,62,64,73
Phyllis Mary YH 578 (sd)	79	Speranza YH 817 (sd)	69,78,82,93		
Piscatorial YH 762 (sd)	77	Spray YH 252 (smack)	44	HMD = His Majesty's Drifter	
Pleiades YH 227 (sd)	69	St. Rollux	32	HMT = His Majesty's Trawler	
Prince Albert (lifeboat)	40,48	Star (coble)	22,28	mfb = motor fishing boat	
Prince Blucher (yawl)	21,23	Storm (yawl)	21,30,34,35,36	Sd = steam drifter	
Propheta (schooner)	37	Stratten (HMT)	77	St = steam trawler	
Prosperity YH 276 (smack)	69	Sunbeam II YH 279 (sd)	79,80		
Puffin YH 414 (sd)	67	Surprise (schooner)	34		
Pytho (brig)	37	Susanna (brigantine)	15		

107. A line drawing sketched by the celebrated Yarmouth naturalist Arthur Patterson to help raise money for the Relief Fund at the time of the 1901 lifeboat disaster. Patterson drew it only four days after the event and as a result included the actual words spoken by Jimmy Haylett at the inquest.